DESIDERATA

DAVID PAUL EICH

Desiderata

A Teenager's Journey to God

IGNATIUS PRESS   SAN FRANCISCO

Cover art © Firstlight/ImageState
Cover design by Riz Boncan Marsella

ISBN 0–89870–858–3
Library of Congress control number 2001089340
Printed in the United States of America ∞

This book was written especially for Catholic teenagers
with the hope that they will keep the Memorare in their hearts
and live accordingly:

Remember, O most gracious Virgin Mary,
that never was it known
that anyone who fled to your protection,
implored your help,
or sought your intercession,
was left unaided.
Inspired with this confidence,
I fly unto you, O Virgin of virgins, my Mother;
to you do I come, before you do I stand,
sinful and sorrowful.
O Mother of the Word Incarnate,
despise not my petitions,
but in your mercy hear and answer me.
Amen.

CONTENTS

ACKNOWLEDGMENTS

I wish to express my appreciation to the contemporary heroes who took the time to open their souls to me as I searched for real stories of real people. Their desiderata is what this book is all about.

Thank you to Brian Bohnett, whose talent, creativity, and design added personality to the work. Thanks to Mr. Robert Polk, who took the time he did not have to edit my writing, my logic, and my theology. It is special when your instructor teaches English and spent four years in the seminary.

Without my Cindy's patience with a husband who disappeared on numerous evenings and weekends to finish the manuscript, this work would have never been completed.

Then of course there are my sons. Though both our boys live in other cities, they regularly call Mom and Dad. And there was not a time when my "guys" did not ask: "Dad, how is the book coming? When will you be done?" Their conversation always ended up with the three most important words in any language. "I love you."

As I finish this section I have a very special young lady I need to thank. To my daughter, Kelly, I owe more than a father's love. I thank her for acting as my consultant when I needed to understand better the trials and tribulations young people her age face. I thank her for her sense of humor, which I badly needed on those days when I was too tired to write, but not too tired to ask for her help. I thank her for her help with organization, corresponding with Mr. Polk, rushing to the post office, and challenging me to live up to what she expects in her dad. But most of all, I thank my daughter for reminding me why I decided to write this book.

PROLOGUE

This book is about a journey. Patterned after the rosary, the reader is invited to "live" each decade of the Joyful, Sorrowful, and Glorious Mysteries. But unlike the rosary, there will be no recitation of the usual prayers. Instead, you will be invited to experience three distinct sections for each mystery.

The first section will introduce those saints whose lives parallel the message being communicated. The beginning of these first sections will be identified with the symbol of the cross.

The second section offers questions and commentary designed to challenge Catholic teens and, to some degree, their parents. The beginning of this section will be signaled with a symbol commonly found on the back of the Immaculate Conception medal.

Section 3 introduces a number of stories of contemporary people whose spiritual journey may delight, surprise, or even shock you. Their symbol, the "anchor cross", is a visual complement to where they have been, where they are, and where they are headed.

To understand better the foundation of this book, one must begin with the rosary. The prayer was reportedly given to Saint Dominic, by the Blessed Virgin Mary, as he was praying to God for the armor he would need to fight heresies against the Church. The power of this prayer was demonstrated on Sunday morning, October 7, 1571, when a badly outnumbered Christian fleet was sailing into battle against the Turks. Pope Pius V had been preparing for the defense of the Church by asking all Christians to say a rosary, pleading for the intercession of the Blessed Virgin Mary. By that afternoon, the Christian fleet was victorious, having destroyed fifty Turkish ships while capturing more than one hundred others. The Christian forces lost only twelve of their galleys. The miracle of the Battle of Lepanto was credited to the power of the rosary. Throughout the centuries there have been similar victories against evil.

Each of the mysteries of the rosary offers a particular virtue. Beginning with the Joyful Mysteries, the first—the Annunciation—in which the Angel Gabriel announced that God had chosen Mary to be the Mother of the Most High, represents the ultimate test in humility. Mary's humility is captured in her Magnificat (Lk 1:46–55). The first three verses set the tone for this beautiful canticle: "My soul magnifies the Lord, and my spirit rejoices in God my Savior, for he has regarded the low estate of his handmaiden. For behold, henceforth, all generations will call me blessed" (46–48). The second mystery, the Visitation, is the story of Mary's visit to her cousin Elizabeth, which demonstrates the gift of charity toward one's neighbor. The Nativity, or the birth of Jesus, is the third Joyful Mystery and sets forth an example of what it means to have the spirit of poverty as evidenced by the poor conditions awaiting our Lord's arrival. In the fourth Joyful Mystery, the Presentation of the baby Jesus in the temple, following Jewish custom, illustrates the virtue of obedience. Finally, the fifth Joyful Mystery, Finding Jesus in the Temple, is a beautiful story on the virtue of piety as Jesus left His Father's house to be with Joseph and Mary. All five mysteries can be found in the Gospel of Luke. (Please note, however, that in the organization of this book's chapters, the author has elected to substitute the word "Epiphany" for Nativity, "Consecration" for Presentation, and "Discernment" for Finding in the Temple. The rationale for this decision will become clearer as the reader delves into Part I, "The Promise".)

The Sorrowful Mysteries evoke different virtues. The Agony in the Garden calls for a true contrition of heart as Jesus honestly cried out to His Father in heaven. The Scourging at the Pillar asks for the virtue of purity as Jesus was scourged in order to cleanse us of our sins. The third Sorrowful Mystery, the Crowning with Thorns, demands moral courage of the type the Savior showed as He accepted the "crown of martyrdom". The fourth Sorrowful Mystery, the Carrying of the Cross, demonstrates the virtue of patience that He showed with his executioners, the weeping women, and the apostles who abandoned Him. And the fifth and final Sorrowful Mystery, the Crucifixion, relates to perseverance, as Jesus completed His passion to the end. The Gospels of Matthew, Mark, Luke, and John detail one or more of the Sorrowful Mysteries.

In the Glorious Mysteries, four different parts of the Holy Bible are used as references. The Gospels address both the Resurrection and the Ascension. The Acts of the Apostles captures what happened at the Ascension and also at Pentecost, when the Holy Spirit inflamed Mary and the apostles. The third chapter of Genesis, the first book of the

Bible, can be seen as relating to the Assumption of the
Blessed Virgin Mary, while the last book of the Bible,
Revelation, supports the belief that Mary was crowned
Queen of Heaven. The Resurrection stands for the virtue
of faith. For if Jesus did not rise from the dead, our faith is
in vain. The Ascension corresponds with the virtue of
hope, as we recognize that though Jesus returned to His
Father, He is with us always. The third Glorious Mystery,
the Descent of the Holy Spirit, calls for the love of God
through the gifts of the Third Person of the Trinity. The
Assumption, the fourth Glorious Mystery, requests devotion to Mary. She is the Queen of Heaven. And the
Coronation, or fifth and final Glorious Mystery, is her
promise for eternal happiness.

    As you read through each chapter, consider the title of
this book: *Desiderata: A Teenager's Journey to God*. The word
desiderata is Latin, the plural of *desideratum*, meaning "something considered necessary or highly desirable". When
Saint Dominic received the rosary from our Lady, he must
have thought that the Mother of God could not have
given her children a better gift.

PART I

The Promise

THE ANNUNCIATION

"I Cannot Promise You Happiness in This Life"

O N February 11, 1858, a fourteen-year-old girl had an experience that would change her life for eternity. On that day, Bernadette Soubirous, a peasant girl from the village of Lourdes in southern France, would experience the first of several visits from the Blessed Virgin Mary. And like Mary before her, Bernadette had a choice. Fortunately, this saint-in-the-making would say Yes to God.

Asked to gather firewood, Bernadette, her sister, and a friend ran down to a wooded area. But Bernadette's asthma did not allow her to keep up with the other girls. Stopping to rest near a grotto adjacent to the city dump, she was startled to see a beautiful lady standing on a bush.

Frightened, the young girl began to recite the rosary. The Lady silently joined in the prayer and then vanished. Bernadette jumped up and raced to find the other girls to share her excitement. From then until March 25, the Mother of God would appear many times to this young French maiden.

Young Bernadette would not realize that her commitment to visit with the "Lady" would lead to personal ridicule by friends and neighbors, embarrassment for her family, and threats from local authorities. Nor did she understand that her decision to return to the grotto would ultimately result in a dramatic career change far from the standard path a poor and below-average student would be expected to follow. Her parents would challenge their daughter's story, scolding her for spreading lies. The city prosecutor promised to punish her if she kept stirring up the populace. And local priests would initially condemn the so-called "visions". But during one of these visions with hundreds looking on, though neither seeing nor hearing, a miracle happened. The place where the Blessed Virgin Mary told Bernadette to dig suddenly produced a stream of water. Hours later a stonecutter, blind in one eye from a work-site accident, washed his face in the stream and just as suddenly had his sight restored. He was the first of many.

Word spread like wildfire. The next day a distraught mother took her dying child to the waters of the grotto, dipped her son in the stream, and was rewarded by the "cry" of a healthy baby. Hours before, this little boy had received the last rites.

Word spread all over France about Bernadette Soubirous and the miraculous waters of Lourdes. Thousands of pilgrims, many sick and some dying, would travel to this remote village hoping to be blessed by God.

But for Bernadette Soubirous, who had become a celebrity to both the faithful and those who wanted to destroy the faith, another decision was waiting. Encouraged by the very priest who had once scolded her for "dancing with the devil", Bernadette would join the Sisters of Notre-Dame de Nevers, an Order dedicated to poverty, sacrifice, and prayer. But even in this environment certain residents were not exempt from sins of envy. Some chose to make Bernadette's life of servitude all the more difficult. Challenging the saint-to-be, they often asked Bernadette if she felt superior because of her so-called worldly fame. Bernadette would respond, "I served as a broom for the Blessed Virgin. And when she no longer had any use for me she put me in my place, behind the door. There I am and there I shall remain."

If this were not enough, Bernadette's health began to deteriorate rapidly as tuberculosis was eating away at her body. Ironically, the same girl who through the grace of God led others to the healing waters would not receive the miracle of Lourdes. Yet Bernadette was quick to remind those who cared for her in her illness of what the Holy Mother had told her: "I cannot promise you happiness in this life, only in the next." And when the end came, Bernadette Soubirous would once again see a vision of our Lady. At that moment the young saint smiled, closed her eyes, and died. She was thirty-five years old.

For Bernadette Soubirous, attention was the last thing she was looking for. Prior to that fateful trip to the grotto, her only aspirations had been to survive her schooling, find a servant-girl position, and have a family. Instead,

Bernadette Soubirous became the spiritual vessel for the establishment of an internationally famous shrine that would draw people from all over the world, and some of these would receive the gift of being healed. And because of Bernadette's obedience to the Mother of God, members of the Church would receive confirmation that the dogma of the "Immaculate Conception", defined only four years earlier, was indeed confirmed by heaven. As a final testament to God's grace, this young peasant girl's body has yet to decompose even though she died more than 120 years ago.

On February 11, 1858, a young teenage girl was invited to attend an annunciation. What Bernadette Soubirous did not know then, but what she knows now, is that she was the guest of honor.

A Whisper in the Womb

Before you were born, God knew you. He knew that this day you would be reading about your annunciation. He understood that you might not understand. So sit back, relax, and let the Holy Spirit sort things out.

Let's begin with a key definition. What exactly is an annunciation? Simply put, it is an announcement or, if you will, a proclamation of an event, like the time when the Angel Gabriel announced to Mary that she was favored by

God. But since we are talking about your annunciation, the question we must ask is: What is worth announcing?

Well, to start with, God loves you enough to invite you to serve others. And though He knows you have potential, He will not force you to make a commitment. If He did, then He would be taking one of His greatest gifts away from you: free will. You also need to know that He expects your emotions to range anywhere from fear to joy, confusion to clarity, surprise to expectation. He knew all this before you took your first breath. And now He knows that you might have a few questions.

But before you begin your dialogue, remember that logic, emotional appeal, or demands of the conscience have no jurisdiction over your right to choose. You can say No. You can argue that the time is not right or the circumstances are not right. You can even protest that God has selected the wrong person for the job. This is only a calling. An invitation. You can reject it. The choice is yours.

"Why Me, Lord?"

Why not? Are you not blessed with certain God-given talents? Does it not make sense that the Creator knows what you have to offer, when, and under what circumstances? Do you think He would ask you to get involved if He thought you would fail? God is calling you for a reason. And though the agenda may be unclear, there is no doubt that it is divinely inspired.

Remember the apostles? How many of those smelly old fishermen do you think really understood what Jesus was asking of them? True, they were captivated by our Lord's charisma, miracles, and storytelling. And a few of them began to question whether or not this "man" was truly the Savior they were waiting for. But even then, they did not realize what sacrifice would be asked of them. They just knew that they were being "called". And they answered.

How about Bernadette? Do you think this young girl had any idea what our Blessed Lady had in mind on February 11, 1858? For that matter, do you think Mary, the Mother of God, knew the ramifications of her Yes when she responded to the Angel Gabriel? Both Bernadette and Mary accepted the invitation on "blind faith", the same faith God is asking of you. It is kind of like the wind. You know it exists. You can feel it. But you cannot see it.

So back to the question: "Why you?" Surely, you think, others are more qualified. After all, Joan of Arc you're not. Besides, what will your friends say? How will your family react? What about teachers, coaches, or neighbors? You are not a hero, someone needing the podium to accept your "due" recognition. Aren't such honors reserved for those who would follow in the footsteps of Mother Teresa?

Funny, isn't it, we come up with so many reasons why we should not get involved, and yet we admire others who do; we worry what others think, while others are often thinking only of themselves; and we let our weaknesses justify why we should not concentrate on our gifts. If only we could trust. Trust in Him who is calling us to His service. Trust that He knows what is best for you just as He knew what was best for the saints.

It won't be easy. But you have heard these words before. For example, the time your coach told you hard work is the price you will pay for victory. Or when your teachers predicted that you will only get out of your studies what you put in. "You reap what you sow!" And God is asking you to sow His glory.

"But What If I Fail?"

What if you do? Is it not possible that this invitation may be a test? What if God merely wants to see if you will accept His challenge? God did that once before, inviting Abraham to sacrifice his son. What if He wants to measure your ability to endure adversity? What if God just wants to see if you understand that one of the Seven Gifts of the Holy Spirit is fortitude? Such a decision takes courage. Conviction. Grace. Prayer.

In a perfect world you would require some guarantee that your involvement is the right thing to do. You need assurances, a safety net. Unfortunately, this is not a perfect world. On the contrary, this is a world filled with contradiction. And maybe that's the point. Perhaps all God is asking is for you to stand up for what is right, what is fair, what is love. Do you not ask as much from family, friends, even strangers?

But if you are truly worried that you might let someone down, ask yourself these questions: Do I really want to say No to the Savior who gave His life for me? Can I turn from a Mother who said Yes without hesitation? Yet the Son of God will forgive you if you choose to walk away. He will wait, hoping that you will hear the call of the Holy Spirit in your heart; hoping that the love God has for you will inspire you to share that love with others; hoping that one day your RSVP will arrive with "no regrets".

"But What's in It for Me?"

What is your reward? Will you be remembered? And who will receive the benefit of your sacrifice? Maybe the answer is "proper pride". If pride is one of the seven sins, then perhaps proper pride is the antithesis of such behavior. Said another way: "To multiply in the lives of others those talents one receives from God."

If God is the author of who you are and the designer of the gifts you have been blessed with, does it not follow that you have both a right and a responsibility to share those gifts with others? Would you not expect the same of those you love and who love you? Must we always get immediate payback for what is expected of us? Is it not enough that the Son of God promised that if you love your neighbor you will spend eternity in heaven?

If this promise is not enough for this world, then perhaps you will just have to settle for having fun serving others while at the same time experiencing a spiritual renewal. If this is not enough to inspire you, maybe your friends will when you notice they are motivated by your actions. Who knows, they may offer to help carry the cross you are so worried about.

So imagine what might happen if you choose to serve. Your decision might inspire e-mail exchanges, family room discussions, and classroom conversations—all because you accepted the invitation to do something that needed to be done.

"Knock and It Shall Be Opened to You . . ."

No matter how hard you try, this "calling" will pick at your conscience. The desire to be adventuresome, daring, a leader, a prophet, will conflict with the status quo. You may tell yourself you do not have time. But you know how much time you are wasting. You may argue that other opportunities will surely surface. Yes. But the chance that you might be turning your back on *the* opportunity will be unsettling. How will you know if you do not try? You will not.

So it all comes back to faith in the Author of life that His invitation is in your best interest and the interests of those He is asking you to serve. Have faith in the fact that He is preparing your banquet. Have faith in His glory, His mercy, His will, and faith that He will be there to help you face your adversaries. Faith that He will give you the grace you need, when you need it, and that your guardian angel will be there to watch over you. Faith that the Holy Spirit will give you the wisdom to discern right from wrong and good from evil.

But regardless of all that has been promised, you still have to make a decision. From the beginning it has been your choice. The only question is whether you are ready to accept your annunciation.

"Because You Missed the Time of Your Visitation . . ."

It was final exams. And once the tests were over David would relax and enjoy the Christmas season knowing that he would not have night classes for the next three weeks. He stopped in at Our Lady Queen of Peace Catholic Church for his daily fifteen-minute visit. David would often visit the chapel before his night classes when he wanted to be alone for some quiet reflection.

But on this particular evening his conversation with God would take a different path. As David prayed, he felt a "presence" that was quite unsettling. Turning around, he saw staring at him a young man about twenty-five with blond curly hair. Knowing that this was a dangerous part of town, David immediately moved his briefcase closer to his right side, so that the stranger would not be able to grab it and run out of the church.

"Is there anything I can help you with?" David asked. The unwanted visitor smiled and said, "Yes, perhaps you can. You see, my wife and our newborn son are waiting in the car, but we don't have any place to stay. Can you help us?" Recognizing the situation as a setup for a handout or worse, David calmly offered, "You know, I'm not from around here, but if you go over to the rectory I'm sure the parish priest would be more than happy to help you, your wife and child." The stranger smiled and nodded a half-hearted "thank you".

Satisfied that the "crisis" was avoided, David turned back to face the crucifix and continue praying. But uncertain of the visitor's real intentions, David looked over his shoulder to make sure the stranger was moving to the back door of the church and out to his car, where supposedly his wife and child would be waiting.

There was only one problem: No one was moving because no one was there! Startled, David jumped up to see where the stranger was hiding. He looked in the pews; he ran to the side door, but it was locked; he ran to the back of the church and went outside. There was no car, no wife, no baby. There was no one. Visibly upset, he grabbed his briefcase and rushed to class, denying all the way that the encounter had ever happened.

David could not concentrate that evening as he played over and over in his mind what had happened. Was he imagining things? Had the stranger really been there? Did he slip out through some other door? No! There was only one way in and out at that hour. Perhaps the time from when David turned his back to when he glanced over his shoulder had been more than just a few seconds. But even if it had been, how could the stranger have raced to the back of the church, jumped in a car, and driven out of sight in such a short time? It was impossible! David was out of answers.

As he was leaving class that night, David cried out in silence. "Lord, I'm terribly confused about what I experienced this evening. But please, if the stranger was You in any way, please give me a sign."

While walking to his car, David noticed an old man sitting on the side of the curb trying to fight the cold. It was not uncommon to see a "street person" in this part of town. Nor was it unusual to see so many students walk past people like this. As David was about to join the crowd, the old man stood up, turned, and said: "Son, could you spare a quarter for a warm cup of coffee? You need not touch my hand, just throw the coin in the gutter and I'll pick it up."

David had the first part of his answer. The second came some time later when he relayed the story during confession. After some reflection, the elderly priest calmly asked, "David, you did say that this event happened just before Christmas; is that right?" David nodded. "And didn't the stranger say that he was new in town, alone with his wife and newborn baby?" Sadly, David nodded again. "Son," the priest said, "that night you were the innkeeper, and there was no room in your heart. That night, you missed your annunciation!"

THE VISITATION

"Amen, I Say to You, As Long As You Did It for One of These, the Least of My Brothers"

I N September 1181, in a small city in northern Italy, a baby was born to a lady named Pica, wife of a wealthy merchant. A few days after the birth of her son, a stranger came to Pica's door asking for alms. Since it was the custom of the times never to turn a beggar from a home where a child had recently been born, the servant of the house let the pilgrim in to have a bite to eat. Perhaps feeding his hunger was not the stranger's only intention. Perhaps he hoped to hold a future saint. The child was called Francis, and one day he would be canonized Saint Francis of Assisi.

As the boy entered his teenage years, he had a lot of

things going for him. He was handsome. He could sing. He was rich. As a result of these "worldly blessings", he soon was labeled a playboy who was always out for a good time. But this young man had another "gift", one that often puzzled his friends. Francis, seeker of pleasure, had the annoying habit of giving both money and fine clothes to the poor.

When Francis was in his late teens, war broke out between Assisi and a neighboring city, which resulted in imprisonment for the popular playboy. This experience eventually led Francis to believe that he was called to be a soldier, a leader of men. Wanting to maintain his image, Francis bought the best military armor money could buy. But his generosity led to his decision to give another soldier his fine uniform, as his comrade could not afford such an exquisite image. Dressed in "hand-me-down" knight's clothing, Francis journeyed off to war. But he never experienced the horrors of battle, as sickness overtook him.

During his illness, Francis had unusual dreams that changed his life forever. In one dream, he saw weapons of pure gold in the shape of a cross. To add further confusion, he saw a beautiful young girl who said, "These arms are for you and your companions." In another dream he heard a voice that asked, "Is it better to serve the Master or the servant?" These puzzling invitations led Francis back to Assisi, where he would eventually give up worldly possessions.

To understand his "calling" better, Francis discarded his royal robes and exchanged them for rags owned by a man stricken with poverty. On another occasion, he chose to overcome his fear of lepers by caring for the physically wretched. Francis would serve God by serving his brother. This vocation fulfilled the young girl's prediction, as Francis of Assisi was later joined by others who shared his ideals and way of life.

Saint Francis of Assisi, product of the secular world, is remembered for many things. With Saint Clare, he founded the Poor Clares, an order of nuns whose life of prayer and poverty paralleled that of the Franciscans. He wrote the famous "Canticle of the Sun", a cherished poem to God that celebrates nature's beauty. And because he refused to give up his dream to have his new order approved, he somehow managed three personal meetings with the Pope. His persistence eventually led to recognition of the Franciscans, some five thousand men, all dedicated to poverty. Francis would care for lepers whose appearance was so gross that even the Saint's fellow brothers would turn from these "untouchables". Francis was also known to preach to the creatures of the forest. It was little surprise that this saint of God was readily approached by birds and animals. And if this were not enough, Francis had repeated visions of Christ and the Blessed Virgin. He even became known as "Brother Francis" by family members of a Sultan whose singular goal was to defeat the Christians during the crusades. But perhaps one of the greatest testimonials of God's love for Francis of Assisi was the "stigmata", by which he physically experienced the five wounds of Christ in feet, hands, and side.

On October 4, 1226, this simple man, who once wished to be a soldier, would himself be carried by knights to Assisi, allowing local townsfolk, fellow brothers, and the Poor Clares to see their beloved Saint for the last time. On his deathbed, Saint Francis would humbly challenge them with these final words, "I have done my part, may Christ teach you to do yours." And then he died.

Saint Francis of Assisi's journey to sainthood began with a stranger's visit. And throughout his life, Francis would visit those no one would have anything to do with. At the end of his life, those who knew him would testify that indeed a saint of God had walked in their midst.

WWJD?

Have you ever wondered why certain teens come into your life without invitation? Did it seem that you were always the one they looked to for comfort? And did you find yourself asking why they did not pester their own friends? What about parents, teachers, counselors? Could these "neighbors" not take the time to listen to this person? And since when did it become your responsibility to lend an ear to her? Besides, she is not like you. Not part of your circle of friends. And speaking of friends, what will they say if they see you hanging around with someone like her? It is almost as if you had a sign around your neck that read, "Open for hearing your problems".

Maybe you think you are being set up. Perhaps this is some kind of joke. After all, everyone knows these people are not your kind. You have nothing in common. And you would prefer to keep it that way. Their problems are really none of your business. Surely others are more qualified to help, to listen, to care, to love. You are too busy anyway. And besides, you would never think of asking anyone for help the way they ask you. The nerve. If you did drop everything you were doing, what would stop them from coming back a second time, third time, or more? Next thing you know they would be telling everyone that you are a friend of theirs!

But is it so hard to listen for a moment? Maybe all they need is a kind word. A smile. Have you not been there before? How did you feel when someone you did not know very well took the time to listen to your problems? Maybe that is why there is something troublesome about this encounter. Conscience perhaps? Could it be you re-member your parents telling you to be kind to others? Was it that religious instructor who said, "Do unto others as you would have them do unto you?" Or maybe you remember what it felt like when you were shunned be-cause someone would not give you the time of day. It hurt. You were angry. Embarrassed.

But perhaps the real reason you do not want to get involved is that you have your own worries, fears, and anxieties. And if so, what if people find out that you are not the big shot on campus that everyone thinks you are? Besides, if you had problems you certainly would not come crawling to them. So what gives them the right to expect so much of you? But that is the point. It is not what they expect you to do. It is what God expects you to do. Something about "love your neighbor." And that includes those who do not measure up to your standards. For all you know, the time you take to reach out to those in need may well make a difference in how God reaches out to you.

Perhaps those asking for your time will turn out to be your best friends. And maybe years from now you will look back on this single event as the best decision you ever made.

You see, one never knows when, how, or why certain people come into our lives. Today's kindness is tomorrow's blessing. And sometimes tomorrow's sorrow is today's apathy. How often have you heard the story of how your parents met? Ask them whom they thought they were going to marry, but did not. Ask them where they thought they were going to live, but could not. Ask either parent to recall what was written in their high-school yearbook about the person "most likely to succeed". Then ask this same parent to set the record straight. You will find that very few teenagers fulfill the prophecy of their peers. Beauty queens too often end up with broken hearts, while many sports heroes are never heard from again. And very often, today's nerd is the same person you will meet at your future class reunions, the one whom all your friends will be talking about, wishing they had treated him better.

So before you reject the classmate, co-worker, neighbor, or teammate, ask yourself a few questions. "What would Jesus do if those asking for your help approached the Lord?" "If you needed help, how would Jesus treat you?" Finally, "How do you know that Jesus did not send these people as a test to see what you would do?" Think about it.

"But When Did I See You, Lord?"

Ever been "touched by an angel"? How do you know? What makes you think that the stranger asking for help is not sent from God? To you he may look like a beggar. He may even be mentally unstable. Whatever his story, it is easy to rationalize that he deserves what he got in life. At least that is the argument used by many to justify their decision to turn away. After all, how many times have you seen undesirables holding signs that proudly state, "Will work for food"? Most agree that such a ploy could be nothing more than a scam to get money so that the desire for liquor or drugs will be satisfied. And what about the inherent risk? You have heard stories where well-intentioned people were misled, even to the point of violence.

You probably think you are too smart to fall for that trick, don't you? Besides, even if the request is legitimate, are not their tears only a watershed for the guilt they have in their heart? It is not your problem that they failed in work, marriage, or life. Whatever happened to the phrase, "you reap what you sow", you ask? If the situation were reversed, would this stranger come to your aid? You bet your life he wouldn't.

But let us suppose the request for help is legitimate. Would it matter that your ages are different? What about ethnic background? If they came from the "wrong side of the tracks", would it make a difference? Is it that difficult to take a moment of your precious time to listen, smile, or love?

Remember, this episode could be a test. I know, the "angel" thing again. You do not want to believe that you have been chosen. But consider this: You do not know why you are being approached, nor do you know the future impact of your present decision. Your choice to help or not help the stranger may be the catalyst for what he will or will not do. Even more directly, your choice may well determine which road you will travel in the future. Simply put, is it not likely that the God who created both of you is waiting to see if you will help His creation?

And if you do, what can you expect in return? Is peace of mind not enough? What about a clear conscience? Or do you require something more? Is it not rewarding enough to know that by helping your neighbor you did the right thing? Do you always need some tangible reward that communicates you did the right thing? Must you receive public acknowledgment that you are a good person as evidenced by your willingness to help? Is such behavior your version of "return-on-investment"? And does it matter that your quest for attention might serve only to embarrass the beneficiary of your so-called generosity?

Whatever you do, never forget that someone is watching. Waiting. Caring. Forgiving. Loving. And you know Who that is. Can you afford not to respond? Do you run the risk of one day experiencing a similar scenario where you will cry out but no one will hear? How would it feel to be the prostitute who would have been stoned to death had it not been for the mercy of her Savior? And speaking of mercy, what if Jesus had ignored the ten lepers, the blind man in the temple, the centurion's slave, and the thief on the cross who asked for forgiveness just moments before he died with Christ? Where would these souls have ended up if the Son of God had chosen to turn His back on those asking for His help?

Remember Lazarus? He was the poor man who begged for food outside the rich man's house. Unfortunately, though the wealthy man had everything, he chose not to share anything with his neighbor. When the rich man died, he found himself in eternal torment begging for a drop of water from the same beggar who now was in the glory of heaven. "You reap what you sow."

Welcome to the Chamber of the Silent

In the twelfth century, a Jewish theologian and physician by the name of Maimonides wrote about eight ways we can choose to help others. With each new level there is a greater call to humility. So the next time you have an opportunity to help one in need, consider the degree with which you want God to remember you.

The first degree: To give with reluctance or regret. This is the lowest degree, a gift of the hand, not of the heart.

The second degree: To give cheerfully, but not proportionately to the distress of the sufferer.

The third degree: To give cheerfully and proportionately, but not until asked.

The fourth degree: To give cheerfully, proportionately, and even unsolicited, but to put it in the poor man's hand, thereby eliciting shame.

The fifth degree: To give in a way that the distressed may know their benefactor, without their being known to him.

The sixth degree: To know the objects of our bounty, but remain unknown to them.

The seventh degree: Is a place called the "Chamber of the Silent", wherein good deposited is secret and from which the poor are maintained with equal secrecy.

Maimonides added an eighth degree, by which he challenged everyone to help prevent poverty before it starts so that no one is forced to hold out his hand. Said another way, the next time someone holds out a hand, remember these words from Saint Francis of Assisi: "Preach the Gospel. Use words if necessary."

"The Sign"

When he got the news, John was ecstatic. The president of the company had just selected this young sales manager to open a new market selling goods and services to school systems across the country. Pulled from all other responsibilities, he was given a travel budget and the time needed to develop the new business.

He began with sales calls at the highest levels. Trade shows allowed him to set up his company's promotion booth, exhibiting his wares to what he hoped would be his future customers. At banquets John was often allowed to speak publicly about the new services he was offering. Friends gave him multiple connections that he knew would surely result in success. But the sales did not come. Connections proved frivolous, potential accounts never called back. Requests for proposals never arrived. Days turned to weeks, weeks to months. Fear of failure was beginning to set in. Facing reality, he decided to meet with the president of the company the following Monday to announce that he had failed and as a result the project should be cancelled. Hopefully, because of his past success, the president would allow him to return to his former position.

Later that day, John received a phone call from a friend who invited him to yet another banquet. His friend implored, "You never know whom you might meet." Reluctantly, the young sales executive agreed to attend the Saturday night function.

The weather that evening was atrocious. Eight inches of heavy snow were forecast, along with high winds. As he got out of his car, he could only shake his head in despair, knowing that few, if any, of the potential clients would dare to venture out in this kind of weather.

As John walked across the street to the banquet hall, a stranger seemed to appear out of nowhere. Somewhat startled, John gruffly asked, "What do you want?" There was no verbal response, only an extended hand holding a business card, with the other hand out asking for a donation. Clearly, this poorly dressed man was a perfect example of those who could not make it in society. Even so, John gave him five dollars, took the card, and stuck it in his shirt pocket. Odd, he thought, "I never bother to help these people. Why on earth would I stop in the middle of a snowstorm and give anything to a stranger?"

The banquet turned out to be a rerun of a bad movie. Same old handshakes, more nameless faces, few promises. "Call me next week." "Sorry, we're not accepting proposals." "We have another supplier." John had heard it all before.

The evening finally ended, and the defeated sales executive returned sadly to his apartment. As he took off his tie, he fell to his knees and cried out to God. "Lord, I've failed. And come this Monday I'm going to admit my failure. But if this is a business I can serve you in, I need some sort of sign. A big sign!"

That Monday morning John selected his very best "funeral" suit for his appointment with the president of the company. Grabbing his wallet and watch, he found his attention drawn to the stranger's card on the floor, which had obviously fallen out of the pocket of the shirt he had worn to Saturday night's affair. John picked up the card and noted the sign language symbols commonly used by the deaf. There was the traditional drawing for "love", "peace", and "hope". Funny, he thought, "I don't see any sign for 'you got the order.' "

Arriving at his office, he was slowly walking to his desk when he was startled to see both his secretary and a work associate running toward him from opposite ends of the hallway. Both individuals arrived almost simultaneously, waiving newspapers in their hand. "What's this?" John asked. The associate blurted out, "Have you seen this advertisement in the San Francisco paper?" Before John could answer, Mary, his secretary, handed him the Philadelphia Sunday newspaper. This paper, like its counterpart three thousand miles away, also offered a similar advertisement asking for interested parties to submit proposals in the very line of business that John had been trying to sell in the past eight months.

Glancing at both papers, John immediately turned to Mary and cried out, "Cancel the appointment with the president. We have business waiting for us." "How can you be so sure?" they both inquired. John then pulled out the stranger's card. You see, both schools requesting a proposal were schools for the deaf!

Today, John heads up a division of a Fortune 500 corporation responsible for more than six hundred million dollars in business. "I need a sign, Lord", he cried out. And the Lord sent John his visitation.

THE EPIPHANY

"Daughter of God, You Must Leave This Village"

R EMEMBER when you were twelve? You could not go far from home without your parents knowing where you were, with whom, and why. Sixth grade had its little challenges. Time-consuming activities ranged anywhere from learning beginning algebra to understanding the consequences associated with failing to do your family chores. You had your friends, hobbies, and dreams. But what you did not have was a clear understanding of who you were and why God loved you. Perhaps you went to church, but, like so many children your age, you probably had no idea why you had to spend one hour a week in prayer. As for the state of the economy, much less the safety of your community, you had little understanding and little desire to understand. After all, you were only twelve.

Jeanne d'Arc, better known in the United States as Joan of Arc, was that same age when she first heard the call. The year was 1424, and the French and English had been at war for more than eighty-five years. In Joan's village of Domrémy, local residents too often experienced the ravages of man's inhumanity to man. The French people continued to await the arrival of "the Maid", whom legend predicted would lead the French people to victory over their enemies. In the meantime, Joan and her family helped neighbors who experienced hunger, sickness, and injury.

One afternoon, while Joan was tending the garden, she heard a voice that said, "Joan, daughter of God, go to church often. Be good and pure. God wants you to do this." On a later occasion, heavenly voices, whom Joan believed to be Saint Margaret of Antioch and Saint Catherine of Alexandria, both martyrs, challenged her with these words: "Joan the maiden, daughter of God, you must leave this village and lead the Prince to be crowned King of France." The young "dauphin", as he was called, was Charles II. Even more unbelievable was a spiritual directive challenging Joan to lead the French army into battle against the English at the city of Orléans. Stunned, Joan cried out, "But how am I, a young girl, supposed to accomplish such a mission?" "Go, daughter of God", was the reply. But Joan did not know where to begin, and for another four years she would ponder the meaning of these words. Even so, her voices would continually come to encourage the teenager to follow the will of God.

In 1428, Joan received another message, instructing

her to visit a French noble who was a supporter of the prince. After some difficulty, Joan finally got an audience with Robert de Baudricourt. But he refused to believe that Joan, a simple teenager, could claim to represent heaven. Joan's request to see the prince was denied. One year later, at age seventeen, Joan of Arc would finally convince the noble to encourage the prince to give her an audience. But another challenge was waiting.

After Prince Charles heard about Joan's pending visit and the spiritual claims behind the request, he designed a test to see whether or not Joan was indeed sent by God. Before Joan entered the court, the prince strategically hid himself in the crowd and instead had a member of his entourage sit in his chair. Joan, upon entering the gathering, looked at the man sitting in the chair and immediately knew that he was not the prince. She then searched the room and, upon finding the true prince, went up and knelt before him. Charles then knew there was something special about the girl. Could she be "the Maid"?

To explore the possibility, the prince had a suit of armor made for Joan, gave her a stallion, and had a special white flag made with the words *Jesus* and *Maria* and picturing God the Father with angels presenting Him a fleur-de-lys. His orders to both Joan and the military commanders were to rescue the city of Orléans from the English. On April 27, 1429, the French army marched to meet their dreaded enemy. During one battle Joan was pierced by an arrow. But after seeing a vision of Saint Michael the Archangel, she struggled back on her horse to lead the French troops to victory. "The Maid" was no longer fiction. As her reputation spread, the French army rallied throughout France to follow Joan of Arc, whose victories would eventually lead to the crowning of the new French king, Charles II.

But Joan's greatest battle was soon to begin. Her "voices" told her that she would be betrayed. Shortly thereafter, Joan was captured by soldiers loyal to England and was sold as a prisoner of war. The charge against "the Maid" was not that of committing war crimes, but rather witchcraft. English clergy attempted to prove that the so-called messengers from heaven were actually soldiers of Satan. Like Jesus before her, Joan faced her false accusers. During the trial the clergy asked her confusing questions on philosophy and theology in order to determine whether her "voices" were agents of evil. Even though her answers contained no heresy, Joan was found guilty of witchcraft and sentenced to be burned alive.

As she was being tied to the stake, she cried out, "I beg all of you here to forgive any harm I have done, as I forgive you the harm you have done to me." As the flames began to rise, Joan asked if anyone had a cross. A friar held up a crucifix so she could gaze at her Savior before her death. Just before she died, she was heard calling on the name of Jesus. And much like the centurion at the foot of the Cross of Christ who remarked, "Truly, this was the Son of God", many English soldiers freely admitted that indeed they had murdered a saint of God. And if the execution was not enough to shake those present, Joan's enemies soon discovered that Joan's heart never burned! One English official, John Tressart, secretary to the king of England, was weeping as he walked away from the fire and remarked, "We are all lost, for we have burned a saint."

Joan of Arc had a role that until the hour of her death she never fully understood. Troubled by her "voices", this teenager could not understand how an uneducated girl could possibly lead an army, much less be responsible for the crowning of a king. But martyred saints Catherine and Margaret and Saint Michael the Archangel all knew why she was called. So too did the soldiers who fought with her realize that she was "the Maid." In the end, Joan of Arc, saint of God, accepted her epiphany.

The Awakening

And just what is an epiphany? An epiphany can be defined as "a sudden manifestation of the essence or meaning of an event". This is similar to when the French soldiers realized that Joan was "the Maid", or when the shepherds knelt before the Child Jesus in the manger. Both groups realized that they were experiencing an event foretold by others. When Joan won the battle of Orléans against the English, it was then that she realized that indeed she was "the Maid". When the Apostle Thomas was present in the upper room at the second appearance of Jesus to the apostles after the Resurrection, Christ invited him to "Put your finger into my hands. Put your hand into my side. Don't be faithless any longer. Believe!" At that moment, a doubting Thomas experienced an epiphany and proclaimed, "My Lord and my God!"

But let's face it, there are few people on the planet

who can claim to have had the privilege of hearing mystical "voices". Generally speaking, the only "voices" a teenager hears and sometimes responds to are those of parents, friends, coaches, or teachers. Voices aside, when was the last time you experienced a miracle?

But even events that are not strictly miracles can seem very strange. A miracle is something that cannot be explained by science. How often have you heard someone state that this or that was just a "coincidence"? "Fate"? "Fluke"? "Luck"? How about serendipity, which relates to accidental discoveries? For those who have faith, "coincidence" and related humanistic terms have no relevancy. And for those who recognize that God is in control, an epiphany is nothing more than a public announcement that one has "awakened".

"The Wind beneath Your Wings"

Do you remember the best day of your life? Would such euphoria have been possible had it not been for the presence of others cheering you on or celebrating your happiness? Said another way, can any "best day" not include enthusiastic support from members of your family or their neighbors? What about your friends or teammates? Did you not share your joy with them? And let's not forget your teachers or coaches. Surely, there have been times when your greatest cheerleaders were those whose primary job was to encourage you to do the best you could in the classroom, on the athletic field, or in the community. Clearly, your "best days" included the presence of one or more of these advocates.

Any person who defends a cause or someone he personally believes in may be designated an advocate. Ideally, the best kind of advocate is one who not only believes in you and the character you demonstrate, but actively has a role in the development of that character. When you were a child, your family had a responsibility to help form those values that would define who you are as a person. As you began your education, your teachers had the duty to help mold the potential within. Coaches, mentors, friends, and neighbors also played a part in your personal development. Unfortunately, there probably were times when those responsible failed in their attempt to set a good example. It happens. And when it does you might well become stronger for the experience. In any case, at one time or another you have had your own personal cheering section made up of individuals who provided the encouragement needed to discover who you really are.

These personal "believers" did what they could to confirm that you had certain God-given talents. They believed in you. They encouraged you. They forgave you. They loved you. And most of all, they had the patience to wait for you to understand why they had such confidence in you. Sometimes you thought you let them down. Though you failed in your eyes, you did not fail in theirs.

When you could not ride your bike without falling, a parent would help you try and try again until the training wheels were unnecessary. When you played your first game, parents, neighbors, coaches, and teammates cheered you on regardless of what you did or failed to do. When you did not do well in school, there were usually one or more teachers who went the extra mile to help you learn the subject. When you let your best friend down, he was still there for you because he was your best friend. Why did all these people stick with you? Do you suppose they saw something in your character that you did not see in yourself? Maybe they held you to a higher standard than others. Better to be challenged than to accept mediocrity.

When Christ was born, it was near the winter solstice, the darkest night of the year. But that night there would be light. The first to understand the magnitude of this event were lowly shepherds. When you were born, God knew who would be the first to know you had potential. Though you have grown in stature and wisdom, there have been times when you were puzzled when a friend, coach, or parent stuck with you after you let them down. Even more curious were students in your class who attempted to strike up a conversation though they did not know you, much less fit your friendship criteria. And talk about embarrassing, what about the times when strangers dared approach you for a handout, or hinted that you would be the ideal "volunteer" for this or that community service.

What did these people see in you that gave them the assurance that you would meet their expectations? Why so much confidence in a person who often had little confidence in himself? Could they be wrong? What if *their* timing was premature? What if you really did not have the "gifts" they thought you had? What if you could not help them? What if . . . ? Oh, you can become your own "doubting Thomas". Or you can just accept the possibility that their invitation is your calling. All you have to do is your best, love your neighbor, and trust God. Whether you knew it then or know it now, there will be times in your life when you will be asked to accept "the wind beneath your wings". And when you do, there will be many who will recognize that this is the time of your epiphany!

The Paul Rundi Story

When Paul Rundi was in middle school, he pondered the possibility that one day he might become a priest. His motivation was the desire to help others. His father, however, was adamant that his son had musical talent that must not be abandoned. Not only could Paul play the organ well, but he could also sing. Not only could he sing, but he also had the ability to make others laugh. With all these abilities added together, Paul Rundi had the potential to become an entertainer.

As Paul entered college, thoughts of becoming a priest were vanishing. His career aspirations changed as he decided to become an engineer. He had good grades. He had the mathematical talent. And as his father suggested, he had a way to make money. But what Paul could not reconcile was the fact that engineering, though an honorable profession, would not allow him to help others directly. Paul changed his career path again and decided to become a psychologist. And though his area of concentration changed, the method for meeting financial obligations did not. Paul put himself through college by singing and playing the organ at local nightclubs.

After earning three degrees, Dr. Paul Rundi was ready to hang out his shingle and earn a living helping troubled children and their parents access the benefits of psychological counseling. As he reached out to moms and dads struggling with child-rearing challenges, it became clear that many parents were actually doing a better job than Dr. Rundi's profession gave them credit for. Recognizing the need to communicate the "good news" about parenting, Dr. Rundi decided to write a book. He knew he could sing and play the organ. He could also make others laugh or, if necessary, counsel them on serious matters. But did he have the talent to become an author? Three books, three videos, and several parenting tapes later, Dr. Paul Rundi knew he had another talent. And that talent eventually led to over two hundred talks a year, four guest appearances on the *Oprah Winfrey Show,* and a unique offer to be the guest host for a morning TV show in a major metropolitan market. In addition, Dr. Rundi was offered the chance to become a radio host. Though he knew this would reach only a fraction of a television audience, he wanted to help others in a special ministry that the TV producers would never accommodate. In the fall of 1994, the Dr. Rundi radio show was born.

Dr. Paul Rundi had a decision to make. Was his destiny in public-speaking engagements; authoring more books; making more videos and tapes; staying in private practice; or becoming a well-known radio talk show host? He did quite well in all areas fulfilling his dream to help others. But Dr. Rundi had another obligation. You see, somewhere along the line, Paul, the one-time would-be priest, fell in love. And Mrs. Rundi loved children more than her husband's celebrity status. In fact, Mrs. Rundi loved children so much that when husband and wife discovered that they could not have any of their own, the first adoption papers were filed. I say the first, because soon there was a second filing, then a third, fourth, fifth, sixth, seventh, eighth, ninth, and (as of this writing) a tenth! Dr. Rundi wanted to help others, and now as father and loving husband, he had the opportunity to put all he had learned and believed into action.

During many of Paul's parenting presentations, he was quick to remind his audience that "parents are God's babysitters." This philosophy was especially evident in the Rundi home, as Mom and Dad chose to adopt what others would characterize as "special needs" children. Two white, one Japanese American, two Hispanic Italians, two other bi-racial, and three black children later, Dr. Paul Rundi could add "father" to his resumé.

From engineer to psychologist, writer to professional speaker, parenting expert to excellent parent, Dr. Paul Rundi had experienced multiple vocations. But regardless of his success, the discovery of his true vocation had not yet materialized. Then one day, Dr. Rundi received a call from a national radio show executive who was looking for a strong Catholic whose pro-family position was compatible with the network's outreach philosophy. Ideally, the show's host would have a clear understanding of Scripture, parenting, and psychology. It would also be helpful if the host had an engaging style capable of holding the listener's attention for up to three hours a day, five days a week. And should the host be published, well, that would be icing on the cake.

On February 15, 1999, Dr. Paul Rundi was about to discover the real reason why he had never become an entertainer, engineer, or TV talk show host. For on that day psychologist, author, professional speaker, husband, and father of ten adopted children would finally experience his calling. Dr. Rundi was about to become a defender of the Catholic faith reaching thousands of listeners across the country in need of the spiritual help he was now prepared to deliver. Today, Dr. Paul Rundi is fast becoming an apologist, someone who argues in defense of a doctrine, policy, or institution.

Has Dr. Rundi completed his vocation? Only God knows if this next step in Dr. Rundi's career path will complete his spiritual journey. But you can bet on this: God knew from the beginning what talents he would bless this man with. God knew how many trials and tribulations Paul would face, as numerous temptations to succeed would be laid at his feet. God knew how hard this devoted husband and father would have to fight to justify the raising of ten children in a culture that says "one child is enough, and two children are plenty." And God knew when and how his servant would be called to reach thousands of listeners around the country. Most important, this same God knew something else. Dr. Paul Rundi was about to experience his epiphany.

THE CONSECRATION

"It Seems the Good Die Young"

IN the late 1960s, there was a popular song entitled "Abraham, Martin and John". Singer/songwriter Dion Di Mucci reminded young people that too many popular heroes died because they stood up for what they believed in. President Abraham Lincoln, a nineteenth-century leader, is best remembered for his stance against inequality. One hundred years later, young protesters would mourn another hero, Dr. Martin Luther King, Jr., who, like President Lincoln, was slain because he stood up for those who were persecuted for the color of their skin. Dr. King will always be known for his freedom marches and famous "I Have a Dream" speech. He championed the belief that all people, regardless of race or creed, are equal in the eyes of God. Songwriter Di Mucci paid a third tribute to President John F. Kennedy, who, like his predecessors, stood up for the dignity of others. In the song's final verse, a question is asked if anyone has seen Bobby Kennedy, younger brother of John, who was also felled by an assassin's bullet. The search for Bobby is remembered with the words, "I thought I saw him walking up over the hill, with Abraham, Martin, and John."

In another time there were three young people whose legacy paralleled the heroes in the song. All three died at an early age; all went against the popular sentiment of the time; and all are remembered for the impact they had on others. Their names were Kateri Tekakwitha, Aloysius Gonzaga, and Agnes. Their stories are a lesson for young people everywhere.

"I Have Thought It Over Long Enough"

Kateri Tekakwitha was born in 1656, in a Mohawk village in upstate New York. She was the orphaned daughter of a Christian mother and Mohawk chief. A smallpox epidemic struck the village when Kateri was four years old, killing her mother, father, and brother. Kateri survived and was adopted by another chief. But the disease had left her skin badly pocked and her vision highly sensitive to light, snow, or sun reflecting on the water. Such impairments led the young Native American maiden to a life in the shadows.

When Kateri was eleven, Jesuit missionaries visited her village. These priests left such a favorable impression on the young girl that she was eventually baptized in the

Catholic faith. The baptismal event occurred on Easter Sunday, April 5, 1676. However, her joy would not last long, as her aunts and adopted father insisted that she prepare to marry, as was the custom for all village girls. But Kateri refused to follow tribal customs. Mocked and ridiculed by other children, punished with hard labor by family members, and constantly tempted by village braves, Kateri soon found herself alone in her commitment to Christ.

In the fall of 1677, Kateri left her people in secrecy, joining other converts at a mission near Montreal, Canada. One of the Jesuits who helped her escape sent a note to the mission superior proclaiming, "I am sending you a treasure; guard it well!" Undoubtedly, the superior agreed, as he waived the waiting period for Kateri to receive Holy Communion. On Christmas Day 1677, twenty-one-year-old Kateri Tekakwitha received the Body and Blood of her Savior.

Kateri lived a life of prayer and sacrifice that others could only marvel about. And though she was known for her piety and hard work, she faced yet another trial. One day a woman accused Kateri of secretly meeting with her husband. Once again rumors and accusations spread. Eventually she was vindicated.

Kateri's final consecration to Christ and the Blessed Mother left no doubt as to her intentions. When she asked for permission to take a vow of perpetual virginity, her spiritual advisor requested that she ponder for three days the decision she was about to make. Kateri left, came back ten minutes later, and said: "I have thought it over long enough. I have already decided what I am going to do. I cannot put it off any longer. I have dedicated my whole self to Jesus, Son of Mary. I have Him for my spouse and only He shall have me as a spouse." On the Feast of the Annunciation, March 25, 1679, Kateri Tekakwitha received Holy Communion and then renounced marriage forever.

Over the next year Kateri observed a life of prayer, fasting, and good works. But during this same year she suffered one sickness after another. On April 17, 1680, the "Lily of the Mohawks" died days before her twenty-fourth birthday. Moments after her death a strange and wonderful miracle occurred. Her face, covered with the ravages of smallpox, suddenly became smooth and beautiful! The miraculous event witnessed by local priests and visitors helped others realize that Kateri Tekakwitha might be a saint of God.

"Blessed Are the Clean of Heart"

Aloysius Gonzaga was born in 1568 to a noble family in Spain. It is said that the first words he spoke were "Jesus and Mary". His parents were personal friends of the king, and because of this, Aloysius grew up in the comforts of royalty. The finest clothes, the best food, superior education, and all the vice one could tolerate could have been his. Not only did he have "connections", but he also had good looks, intelligence, and the benefit of being his father's favorite. So much did his father admire his son that young Aloysius was promised a commission in the king's army.

But Aloysius had a different calling. From the earliest time in his youth, both his brother and mother noted how pious Aloysius was, especially when it came to receiving

Holy Communion and attending Mass. Before he entered his teenage years, young Aloysius consecrated his perpetual virginity to God.

Such a vow promised to be especially difficult to keep because his popularity and handsome appearance soon became the talk of the Spanish court. Further, the society he lived in too often promoted early sexual encounters for young men of nobility. But Aloysius was adamant. He would not tolerate immorality, drunkenness, or taking the name of the Lord God in vain.

Aloysius had other traits that would separate him from his peers. He chose to "dress down", avoiding any class differentiation. He avoided fancy foods, partly because of a kidney disorder, but mostly because he wanted to practice the discipline of fasting. And there was one other curious thing about Aloysius. The young man who had everything going for him in secular society wanted most of all to become a Jesuit priest!

"I forbid you to become a priest", his father thundered. In his father's mind, the thought that his eldest son, one who caught the attention of high society, would give up everything for a life of sacrifice was absurd. And for a time, Aloysius was made to play the part expected of royalty. But the prayer, sacrifice, and love of both his mother and younger brother would protect this future saint from compromising his desire to serve God.

Finally, the day came when his father surrendered to the wishes of his son. Aloysius was sent to Rome to join the Jesuits as a novice. Exchanging his fine tailored clothes for the simple habit, Aloysius Gonzaga entered into the life of God's service.

In those early days, Aloysius was quick to volunteer for

the dirtiest jobs. He fasted constantly even to the point where his superior became concerned for his health. That concern would soon prove prophetic.

In 1591, the "black death" was killing tens of thousands of people in Europe. Aloysius answered the call by volunteering to work in the local hospital caring for the sick and dying, even though he knew that the likelihood of his catching the dreaded disease was very high. At the age of twenty-three, Aloysius Gonzaga went to meet his God. At the hour of his death in his last spoken words he called upon the holy name of Jesus.

Saint Aloysius Gonzaga's example set the tone for generations of young people who have needed the courage to stand up to society's temptations. How many friends do you know who would be willing to give up living in the most expensive neighborhood, wearing the finest clothes, receiving the most prestigious education, and attending an unlimited number of pleasure-seeking parties? How many friends do you have who would gladly give up the best life has to offer in order to serve those who have nothing to live for? And, finally, do you know many in your generation who love God so much that they are willing to remain virgins for life? Such humility and sacrifice is the reason why Saint Aloysius Gonzaga is now universally recognized as the patron saint of youth.

"Mother, Father, Have Courage"

Some thirteen hundred years earlier another young person, like Kateri Tekakwitha and Aloysius Gonzaga, was faced with a difficult decision. Agnes was born in Rome in the year 291, during the time of Christian persecutions. Though her mother and father were themselves Christian, they dared not publicly demonstrate their faith for fear of Roman judgment. Both parents were concerned that one day their daughter's love of Jesus would bring her death.

That day came as the son of a high Roman official approached the beautiful Agnes and asked for her pledge to marry him. Agnes politely informed her admirer that she was betrothed to another. Heartbroken the young man returned to the palace, where one of the servants informed his father that the reason his son had been rejected was because Agnes was a Christian and therefore in love with Jesus Christ.

The boy's father flew into a rage and threatened Agnes' parents that if their daughter did not accept his son's proposal, he would turn the young girl over to the authorities, and she would be condemned for being a Christian. Her parents' grief was met with courage as Agnes proclaimed, "Mother! Father! I will not betray the faith you have given me even if it means suffering and death!"

Because of her faith, Agnes was led to the arena, where she was told to worship the pagan gods. Instead, the young girl made the sign of the cross! With this refusal, a Roman judge ordered her to be confined in a house of prostitution, where she was publicly stripped and threatened by a mob of young men. As the would-be rapists approached Agnes, an intense light covered her nakedness and forced back her adversaries, one of whom was struck blind. According to tradition, after Agnes prayed for him, his eyesight was restored. This young man eventually became a Christian. Dragged back to the arena, Agnes was condemned to die at the stake. But as the wood around her body was set on fire, the flames parted and Agnes was left unharmed. Cries of "away with the witch" echoed throughout the crowd.

In frustration and fear, the Roman prefect ordered Agnes to be killed. According to one account, as the executioner trembled, Agnes was heard to say, "Take me, O Lord, death is really life, the sweet life of eternity. Take me, O Lord."

Agnes died at the tender age of thirteen. Her death had such an impact on the early Christian communities that the name Saint Agnes is mentioned in the same breath with the greatest saints of the Church during the First Eucharistic Prayer at Mass. Saint Ambrose, a Doctor of the Church, captured the beauty of this teenage saint when he wrote, "This child was holy beyond her years and courageous beyond human nature."

Agnes, Aloysius, and Kateri "set the bar" for future generations who travel the road to sainthood. Along the journey, commitment, courage, and sacrifice will be demanded of those who wish to "consecrate" themselves to the Cross.

"You've Got to Be Kidding"

I know. The likelihood that you or any of your friends would be willing to "stick out your neck", much less give up friendships, good times, or money-making opportunities, is slim. But is that what God is really asking of you? Or is He simply suggesting that if you have faith, then the grace necessary to follow the path He has chosen will be there when you need it? Said another way, would God test you beyond what He knows you can handle?

So how do you know just what you can handle? Well, let's start with the basics. By making a commitment to the Holy Spirit you are simply inviting the Author of all graces to guide you in everything you think, do, or say. By making a commitment to Jesus, Son of God, you are serving the Lord who gave His life for you. By making a commitment to the Father, you are giving back to God what all sons and daughters are called to do. This same God will never abandon you.

Remember Saint Paul? He was the arrogant hunter of Christians who himself became the "hunted". After participating in the execution of Saint Stephen, Paul was on the road to Damascus when he was struck by a blinding light and thrown from his horse. As he lay startled, he heard a voice from the heavens ask, "Paul, Paul, why are you persecuting me?" Paul then asked, "Who are you, sir?" "I am Jesus whom you are persecuting", said the voice. From that moment on, Saul of Tarsus, later known as Paul, became a great missionary in the Church. Paul was called to stand up publicly for what he believed in. He was ridiculed, condemned, and eventually put to death.

Sometimes the "lightning bolt" has a different impact. Take the case of the young executive who was driving his Jaguar down a suburban street when all of a sudden a brick came flying right into the passenger side door. "Whack!" Stunned, the owner of the Jaguar immediately pulled over to see who had dared to throw something at his prized possession. He jumped out of the car and was startled to see a young boy standing near a tree crying. "Did you throw that brick?" the executive asked. "Yes, sir", the boy timidly answered. "Just what did you think you were doing? Do you know what this stupid little act of yours is going to cost?" The young boy shook his head and then began to sob. "Please, mister, I'm sorry; I didn't know what else to do", he pleaded. "I threw the brick because no one would stop."

Tears began streaming down his face as he pointed around the tree. "It's my brother", he said. "He rolled off the curb and fell out of his wheelchair, and I can't lift him up." Sobbing, the boy asked the executive, "Would you please help me get him back into his wheelchair? He's hurt, and he's too heavy for me."

Moved beyond words, the driver tried to swallow the rapidly swelling lump in his throat. He lifted the young man back into the wheelchair and took out his handkerchief and wiped the scrapes and cuts, checking to see that everything was going to be okay. "Thank you, and may God bless you", the grateful child said to him.

The man then watched the little boy push his brother down the sidewalk toward their home. Once the boy and his brother disappeared, he slowly walked back to his Jaguar. The executive never did fix that dent in the door. He chose to leave the damage, as a reminder not to go through life so fast that someone has to throw a brick at you to get your attention.

Again you ask: When will God get my attention? How will He get my attention? And what will happen if I choose to ignore Him? Only God knows the answer to when, how, and why. God may ask you to take risks. You may have to proclaim your faith publicly. It may cost you some friends. You may be singled out on the team. You could get a lower grade if the situation demanded that in conscience you must challenge your teacher. Even some family members may question your motives.

But your journey to the Father, the Son, and the Holy Spirit will bring with it new friends, new gifts, and a different kind of wealth. You will discover the talents you have always had. Your confidence will soar as the Holy Spirit soars in you. You will find that you are not in this commitment for honors, awards, titles, status, or gifts. No, you made this commitment for Him who gave you a chance to love Him and love your neighbor.

It is really that simple. You heard God calling because you smiled. You heard His call because you held out a hand to someone in need. You heard the call because you forgave someone. You hear God's call because of faith, love, and charity. And are not these three virtues what God asks of you? Is this not how Jesus set an example as He challenged us to have faith the size of a mustard seed; hope because Jesus bore the weight of the Cross; and love, the gift for one's neighbor? For when you love both God and your neighbor, you will come to understand just how much others need you. You will experience how many opportunities there are to love and what is expected of you to fulfill that command. Then and only then will you come to understand that this is the time of your consecration!

"Promise You Won't Leave Me"

On January 3, 1970, a sixteen-year-old Miami girl named Edwarda lapsed into a diabetic coma. Moments before this happened, she turned to her mother and pleaded, "Promise you won't leave me, will you, Mommy?" Now, more than thirty years later, her mother, Kaye O'Bara, is still keeping her promise. And that promise has meant that she has had to attend to her daughter's needs every two hours, twenty-four hours a day, three hundred sixty-five days a year.

Edwarda has been labeled "vegetative" because of her inability to respond, move, or feel sensations. Her blood must be drawn every few hours, blood sugar checked, insulin injected, saliva suctioned, body shifted, turned, pampered, bathed, and fed. Food is blended and drained into a stomach tube every few hours to ensure that she gets the necessary daily calories.

Added to the medical necessities is the loving care Kaye gives her daughter. Mom washes, brushes, and braids her hair, strokes her face, kisses her forehead, and speaks softly to her child. Asked if she ever tires, Mom laughs and says, "Oh, honey, I don't need caffeine; old-fashioned love keeps me going." "What I do is not a burden, it's an honor", she says. "I asked God for two daughters, and I didn't put restrictions on it." That sums up the promise she made both to her daughter and to God. Some feel sorry for Kaye. Kaye's response: "Pity kills people."

Science cannot explain the power of this mother's love, for Edwarda has been in a coma some thirty years longer than the typical comatose patient. As a result some have criticized Kaye for not letting "nature take its course". To do so would mean that the same mother who promised her daughter to remain with her always would have to starve her child to death. Instead, Kaye O'Bara has chosen to keep her word with selfless compassion rarely seen in this world.

And that is the point. Kaye will tell you what the late Cardinal Bernadin told her: "Edwarda is a 'victim soul'." (This title describes one who makes a choice to suffer on behalf of others needing divine graces in their lives.) Kaye believes that her daughter's sufferings had a role in recent healings of children with cystic fibrosis, a disease with no known cure. Kaye also maintains, "The Blessed Mother visits me three or four times a week."

Regardless of what one cares to believe about this private revelation, there are several truths that cannot be ignored. Edwarda is alive today despite medical predictions to the contrary. The story of a mother's love has captured the attention of the national press at a time when it is considered more convenient to reject children whose physical condition does not meet society's standards. On the day this mother made her promise to her daughter, an act of consecration was sealed among Jesus, Mary, and one Kaye O'Bara.

THE DISCERNMENT

"Father, Forgive Them; for They Know Not
What They Do"—Lk 23:34

IN the middle of the sixteenth century a ship set sail
from England for Italy. Among its cargo was a beautiful
statue of the Madonna.

The seamen on board were instructed to deliver "Our
Lady of Graces" to Naples, a Catholic city on the Italian
peninsula. As the ship neared its destination, a strong storm
gathered, forcing the crew to take shelter in the small
Italian seaport of Nettuno. As soon as the storm quieted,
the crew again sailed for Naples. But again the storm
struck, forcing the ship back to Nettuno's port. A third
time the seas calmed and the sailors launched their ship.
When the storm returned, the crew immediately knew

that the Madonna was to remain forever in Nettuno. Some
350 years later, the citizens of Nettuno would come to
understand why their community had been chosen to
house this tribute to the Mother of God.

Maria Goretti, the oldest of six children, was born on
October 16, 1890, in Corinaldo, Italy. Her father worked
for a landowner, while her mother cared for the children.
When Maria was nine years old, her father died of malaria.
Maria took over the housework, quietly accepting responsibility for the younger children, cooking, cleaning, sew-
ing, and shopping for the family in the nearby town of
Nettuno. It was in this village where Maria visited the
shrine of Our Lady of Graces, where she attended Mass
and received her First Holy Communion at the end of
May in 1902.

Maria had chestnut hair and hazel eyes, and she was
graceful and slender. Her mother would later recall that,
other than her habit of praying frequently at a chapel
down the road, there was nothing particularly unusual
about her daughter. Other adults in the village often
noticed that Maria loved receiving Holy Communion, and
she wore a rosary around her wrist.

Before Maria's father died, he made a partnership with
another poverty-stricken family who shared living quarters
and work responsibilities. Unlike the Gorettis, the Serenelli
family had many troubles. Mrs. Serenelli attempted to
drown her own son, Alessandro. His father paid no attention to the boy at all.

As Maria approached her teenage years, Alessandro,
who was six ears older, became obsessed with the young
girl. On several occasions Alessandro made inappropriate
advances, suggesting that Maria give in to his sexual desire.

Maria often had to push her aggressor away or avoid him. Though the threats continued, Maria never told her mother, as the daughter did not want to cause more stress in her mother's life.

On the morning of July 5, 1902, Alessandro left his duties in the field and proceeded to the farmhouse where he knew Maria was caring for her youngest sister. Driven by lust, Alessandro violently grabbed Maria in the kitchen and began to rip at her clothing. Maria refused to submit to her attacker, who, in a fit of rage, stabbed her fourteen times in the heart, lungs, and intestines. "My God! My God! I'm dying, Mamma!" were the sounds that awoke Maria's baby sister. Hearing the younger child cry, Maria's mother rushed to the house, where she found her daughter in a pool of blood.

Maria was rushed to the hospital, where she lay in excruciating pain for over twenty hours. The surgeons, who worked feverishly to save her life, would later recall how astonished they were that such a young girl with fourteen serious stab wounds could live so long. As she lay dying, a local parish priest gave Maria the last rites. It was during these final minutes that the fate of her killer, Alessandro, was sealed for all eternity. Asked if she could forgive her assassin, Maria replied, "Yes, for the Love of Jesus I forgive him . . . and I want him to be with me in paradise. May God forgive him, because I have already forgiven him." Gazing at the image of the Mother of God, Maria Goretti died on July 6, 1902. She was not yet twelve years old.

Alessandro was sentenced to thirty years in prison, which was the maximum allowed for a minor under Italian law. Unrepentant, he was placed in solitary confinement for three years, where he began to sink into depression. One night while he was sleeping, Alessandro had a dream in which he saw Maria dressed in white and standing in a beautiful garden. She was holding fourteen lilies and offered them to Alessandro. As he took the bouquet of flowers, each was transformed into a shining white flame representing the fourteen stab wounds Maria had received from him. Shortly thereafter, Alessandro asked to speak with the bishop to confess to the murder of Maria.

After twenty-seven years, Alessandro was released from prison, and he arranged a meeting with the mother of the young girl to beg forgiveness for what he had done to her daughter. Mrs. Goretti replied, "Maria has forgiven you. Must I also not forgive you?" This ultimate act of reconciliation occurred on Christmas Eve. Hours later, mother and murderer attended Holy Mass and received Communion together.

The culmination of Maria Goretti's story occurred on June 24, 1950, in Rome, where the Holy Father, Pope Pius XII, canonized the youngest saint in the Church. Though more than fifty thousand people were in attendance, the largest gathering ever recorded, one soul was quietly praying in a monastery several miles away, where he remained until his death.

"What Is Truth?"

It is amazing how many debates could be settled by answering the simple question "What is truth?" Ever since Pilate scoffed at Jesus during our Lord's encounter with the Roman procurator, the answer to that simple question seems to have eluded every generation over the past two thousand years. From border wars to constitutional debates, backyard arguments to lovers' quarrels, the search for simple honesty has proven to be a difficult journey for those of us who believe that the commandment "Thou shalt not bear false witness against thy neighbor" was not simply a suggestion.

For young people, the search for truth usually begins with close friends, a parent, coach, teacher, or someone else whom they admire. In any case, all you are asking is that they be honest with you. The same can be said for decisions you have to make involving your behavior. If you believe there is a difference between right and wrong, and that there is hence a need to make proper judgments, then you have the "gift" of conscience, that inner sanctum where moral warfare is governed by the agents of good or evil. And should you accept the theory that both sides are fighting for your attention, you must also accept the responsibility for listening to one side or the other, which may determine who wins the battle for your soul.

Furthermore, "spiritual warfare" is more than just avoiding evil. It is also a call to action to set an example for good. And your decision to "stand up for what you believe in" may well demand that you take center stage when those you love, those you do not, and those you do not know stand ready to pass judgment on what you say, do, or fail to do.

What will you say? How will you act? How will the crowd react to you? Will they think you are crazy? Judgmental? Insensitive? Will they demand that you be enrolled in the next "conflict resolution" training session? Or might they simply admire your honesty? Anyone who dares to go against the popular position will surely generate discussion. Friends and strangers will ponder your conviction, behavior, and courage. But whatever their conclusions, they will recognize that something is occurring in your life. Something has erased, or at a minimum reduced, the fear often associated with such actions.

You may look for allies and find none. You may wait patiently for your mom or dad to defend your behavior and be disappointed. You may experience what Jesus experienced when so many of His friends walked away from His words and convictions. But someone has got to take a stand. Why not you? If you become the "spark", then maybe others will follow, take your advice, and ultimately take action for the greater good. And if they do, if you do, perhaps a revolution for truth will begin. Wouldn't such an outcome be a refreshing change?

Should you choose to walk away from "truth", what is to stop others from following your decision? And if they do, is not such behavior the reason why so many young people end up choosing the wrong path in life? Yet, many of these same followers would not blame you if you quit. It is better than failing later. Better to walk away than lose friends. Better to follow the crowd than be "branded" as some kind of moral radical.

But something is calling you. Is the "burning bush" stirring the fire in your soul? Are you attracted to the lyrics in a song, a painting on the wall, a parent's wisdom, or the memory of a friend? Does the reason you are hesitating have anything to do with the conscience God has blessed you with? Do you think it is coincidence when the times of greatest stress often occur when you have to make a choice? Imagine what it must have been like when Jesus wept in the garden hours before He was to be crucified. All He was asking was the "right" to avoid being tortured to death for someone else's behavior.

Is it time to see what you can do for Him? Is it time to answer the call to courage? Is it time to set an example for others? Is it time to follow the Way, the Truth, and the Life? If it is, then it is also the time of your discernment.

Character . . . What You Do When No One Is Looking!

You have heard the pronouncement: "What we need is a return to family values." The theme has been stated in countless media reports, magazines, and television talk show discussions. Parenting experts sell "family values" books and tapes promising the magical pill needed to ensure that today's young people grow up to be responsible citizens. Consultants increase their income by selling seats to executives who attend business ethics courses.

Company leadership hopes to see a reduction in immoral decisions currently infesting their organization. Military generals are redesigning "boot camp" programs to ensure that the latest recruits have some semblance of a moral foundation. Meanwhile, national politicians agree to spend tax dollars on "civility" courses so that Republicans and Democrats can learn to be nice to each other.

So if "adults" cannot control their behavior, what right do they have to expect young people to control theirs, you ask. Before we start a national movement attacking parents and other authorities, let's ask ourselves a few questions. Who is the ultimate authority? God! Who gave us the rules we are supposed to live by? God! Who is responsible for our freedom to choose? God! And who so loved the world that He gave His only begotten Son? God! So if God is the answer, then I must ask: "Why would you choose to offend Him who gave you life, free will, and the chance to be with His Son in glory?"

Assuming you have chosen not to offend God, may I suggest that to strengthen your character, you must be able to tell the difference between right and wrong, good and evil. This trait is called discernment. Simply put, it is the ability to make wise decisions. The following is a list of other "character" builders:

- Modesty—Personal regard for how one dresses, speaks, or acts.
- Appreciation—Awareness of how much one has been given by God, parents, and others.
- Responsibility—Willingness to accept consequences of both good and bad decisions.
- Humor—Ability to enjoy life and to laugh, especially at one's own humanness.

- Forgiveness—Ceasing to feel resentment against another because of a wrong committed.
- Honesty—Respect for the "truth" and a willingness to act accordingly.
- Self-Discipline—Controlling behavior or desires for personal welfare or the welfare of others.
- Dependability/Reliability—Being worthy of trust and confidence.
- Courage/Conviction—Ability to face difficulties or to stand strong in one's personal beliefs.
- Stewardship—Giving of time, talent, or money to organizations or to persons in need.
- Self-Respect—Appropriate confidence in one's own worth as a human being.
- Obedience—Acknowledging rules and limits and the authority of others to enforce them.
- Forbearance—Ability to delay gratification and/or accept difficult circumstances.
- Sanctity-of-Life—Full acceptance that all human life, from conception to death, is sacred.
- Work Ethic—Practicing the moral virtue of hard work and diligence.
- Tolerance—Recognizing and respecting different races, religions, cultures, and customs.
- Humility—Appropriate reserve toward the recognition of one's talents and blessings.
- Fidelity—Faithful to obligations, duties, observances, or vows.
- Kindness/Compassion—A sensitivity/considerate action toward those in hardship or pain.
- Temperance—Self-control in managing resources or avoiding excess behavior and life-style.

- Justice—Fair treatment for all in education, health, economic, and criminal arenas.
- Family Loyalty—Defending and honoring one's family, their roots, traditions, and customs.
- Perseverance—Pursuing an endeavor in spite of counter influence or discouragement.

All of these character traits form a "blueprint" for giving glory to God. However, there is another trait that will help you even more. FAITH! Having the spiritual foundation necessary to trust God, His principles, and the eternal hope He offers will go a long way in this world and prepare you for the next!

From Contradiction to Conversion: Danny's Story

His father came from a broken home; his mother, from a privileged family. Together, Danny's mom and dad raised nine children, all of whom were sent to Catholic school. Danny was the second youngest child, growing up in a poor neighborhood where the color of his skin was in the minority, and violence was the rule of the day. Looking back, Danny likens his environment to what today's ghetto children affectionately call "the Hood".

Before he was thirteen, Danny had been beaten, robbed, and offered numerous chances to engage in immoral activities. Drugs, girls, and stolen goods rounded out his daily "temptation menu". Two of the boys who constantly tried to enlist Danny in their life-style met an unfortunate end. One was murdered. The other is serving a life sentence in prison. At his young age, Danny knew two things. First, stay away from evil; second, do not judge others. This interior strength would serve him later.

Danny had another challenge in his life. His dad was an alcoholic. And though Danny was the "apple" of his dad's eye, he, like his eight brothers and sisters, experienced the daily wrath of this troubled man. Too often, the primary target of his father's anger was Danny's mother. On one occasion, his mom was feeling sorrowful because a neighbor woman had just lost a child during labor. Danny's dad took this opportunity to accuse his wife of being the direct cause of the infant's death. Such outbursts slowly but surely began to destroy the family.

When Danny was only eleven, his older brothers and sisters got into drugs. Though Danny initially avoided the temptation, he finally began to follow in their footsteps. By the time he turned fourteen, Danny was taking cocaine, and as a dealer, he was making a 25 percent profit on the sale of marijuana. Though evil was all around him, Danny never stopped talking to God. Just as he did as a child, the young drug dealer would still say his nightly prayers, often thanking God for his life, troubled as it was. He never abandoned God, and God never abandoned him.

By the time Danny entered high school he was a seasoned "hustler", streetwise beyond his years. This experience, coupled with the daily disruptions in his family, could have easily destroyed Danny's chance to utilize his

God-given talents. Two such talents were his athletic and academic abilities. Both would allow him to live another life.

He set records in track, played on a championship football team, and was an exceptional first baseman. In addition to his athletic prowess, Danny was also an outstanding student. His studies came easily. From coaches to athletes, teachers to students, all liked and respected the young man who came from "the other side of the tracks". They knew he had much to offer. What they did not know was that he had much to suffer.

The situation with Danny's father was getting worse, as the alcohol was destroying the man's body, family, and soul. Danny's sister left home; there were physical fights between his dad and his older brother; and there were continuous verbal attacks against his mom. Even so, Danny had dreams. He wanted to go to college. He wanted to be a doctor. He wanted to help others. But Danny wanted something else. He wanted to save his father.

During this dark time in his life, Danny would still commune with God. He would go to Sunday Mass and receive Holy Communion. He would take long walks in the woods and have conversations with his Creator. He would lie awake at night and ask, "Is God still there?" The answer was always, YES! Though Danny could have easily blamed God for all he was experiencing, he chose instead to accept responsibility for doing good. He also told himself that God was never angry with him, because playing hard, studying hard, and partying hard were all part of His creation.

Although Danny gave up using and selling drugs before he went away to college, he did not leave his "cross" behind. One day his mother had to be rushed to the hospital for a bleeding ulcer. That was the first time Danny had ever seen his mother weak. The sight broke his heart. To add to the sorrow, Danny witnessed his father verbally assaulting his mother as she lay in the hospital bed crying. It was then that Danny realized that one of two things would happen: His father would either kill his mother or kill himself. Or maybe both.

The hour had come. Danny knew that except for him and his mom, all members of the family had given up on their dad. Returning home, Danny confronted his father. "Dad, have you seen what you've done to your family?" he asked. With those words, his dad began to cry. "Son," his father responded, "I am a dead man." With that, Danny left and returned to college.

But Danny could not concentrate. Trying to study was ineffective as the words of his father kept piercing his conscience. It would have been so easy to give up. Instead, Danny went to the chapel, looked up at the crucifix, and said, "God, you've got to do something." Suddenly, he heard these words in his heart: "Consider it done!" Startled, Danny began to challenge the interior voice. "No, you don't understand." A second time he heard, "Consider it done." At that moment, Danny knew his prayer had been answered.

He immediately ran to his girlfriend's room and shared the experience with her. She could have easily ridiculed her boyfriend, but she was a Christian whose love of God and understanding of the Bible helped to encourage Danny to take the next step in the saving of his father's soul.

Danny moved his mother out of the home. Within months, his father stopped drinking, returned to Mass, and, once again, started reading the Holy Scriptures. He gave money to the missions. He wrote to the family, begging forgiveness for all he had done and failed to do. And he would bless Danny by tracing the sign of the cross on his forehead. He was a changed man. Soon thereafter, Danny's mom moved back home, where she was greeted with gifts and the love and respect she had sought for twenty years.

Shortly afterward, Danny's dad had a stroke that took away his speech. The once troubled man speculated that his affliction was God's way of punishing a man who had used his mouth to curse his family. Danny's dad understood how the father of Saint John the Baptist, Zechariah, felt when he was struck silent for refusing to believe the angel's announcement that he and his wife, Elizabeth, were going to have a son. The angel proclaimed: "I am Gabriel, who stand in the presence of God. I was sent to speak to you, and to bring you this good news. And behold, you will be silent and unable to speak until the day these things come to pass, because you did not believe my words, which will be fulfilled in their time" (Lk 1:19-20).

God's promise to Danny had its proper time. Before his father died, he had returned to his faith. And Danny's father was not alone. Because of the dramatic change in his heart, another soul was saved. Danny's uncle not only turned back to God, but he became a Catholic after witnessing the miracle in his brother's life. As for Danny, who was now boxing for his college team, he saw God as his "corner man", helping him to stand up to trials he would face, such as when he learned his best friend had died, or when his girlfriend broke up with him.

Danny's Hour

Danny had another revelation: God was now going to deal with him. From that moment, the smoking stopped, the drinking stopped, and the self-gratification ended.

One day, as Danny was jogging along the riverbank, he heard God's voice in his heart: "Start now." Danny knew his duty to serve God must begin, not after he graduated from college, not after he started his medical profession, not after he was financially secure. No, God was demanding Danny's conversion, now! Danny knew he could not wait until he was forty. He knew God had a plan for him. He just had to discover what that plan was.

At first he pondered writing Christian letters as Saint Paul had done. He knew he had both a desire and a gift to evangelize about his profound love for Christ, and, as a result, he joined an ecumenical Christian group. One night as the group was praying, Danny had an overwhelming sense of the presence of God. Suddenly, one of the fellows who was praying with Danny said, "You know what? I just heard God say to you, 'Welcome home, son!' " Danny was startled. He now knew what Jesus meant when He spoke about the "prodigal son".

Others saw the change in Danny. In one situation, a teacher and her entire class witnessed Danny defending the gift of "discernment" in his interpretation of what a Shakespearean character should, or should not, have done. When the class finished, a student asked, "Are you a Christian?"

Danny started praying two hours a day. He read the Scriptures. He fasted. He heard interior messages regarding his family. One message involved his oldest brother,

William. Danny heard God say that He wanted this brother to return to the faith. Danny immediately began to say many prayers for this member of the family. A short time later William confided in Danny that God had spoken to him during an almost fatal accident. When Danny asked his brother what words he had heard, his brother said: "William, I want you back." William, like his brother Danny, had returned home.

A second brother would experience the power of prayer. Again, Danny had an interior message from God asking that he now concentrate on his brother Terry. Danny's prayer would be answered. While visiting Terry, Danny finally got up the courage to tell his closest brother that God also wanted him back. "Who told you this?" Terry demanded. "God", Danny said. It was then that Terry confided that the words he had just been told had been in his head for a week. Terry now prays regularly, attends daily Mass, and invites the clergy into his home.

A third brother was about to experience the healing power of God. Brandon was the wild one. He had been in trouble most of his life, but God, and His servant Danny, never gave up on him. For six years, Danny prayed for this troubled man. One day, Brandon casually mentioned to Danny, "I think God has a purpose in my life." A short time later, Danny was praying when he felt an urgent need to focus on his brother Brandon. Danny heard God say: "Now is the time." A few hours later, Danny called home and learned that his brother had been in a serious car accident at the exact moment when he was praying for Brandon. Danny rushed to his brother's side, but before he could ask how he was feeling, Brandon said: "Danny, do you remember when I said God has a purpose for me?"

Danny nodded. "Well, now is the time!" Another brother had come home.

Medicine, Missionary, or Marriage?

Danny had some decisions to make. Should he continue to pursue his studies in preparation to become a doctor? Should he explore his desire to be a missionary? Should he become a priest? What did God want? The answer would soon follow.

Danny was drawn to an ecumenical missionary group. The organization seemed to offer him the career path he was looking for as they frequently sent Christians to missions all over the world. Interestingly, this group required their members to promise to abstain from sexual intercourse. For Danny, celibacy was compatible with another calling he thought he had. Danny wanted to be a priest. But his new career track had complications, as the missionary group did not want priests among them. When Danny shared his intentions, the organization's leadership delayed asking Danny to leave. Instead, they inquired if he would postpone his decision and accept a tour of duty in Costa Rica. Danny agreed.

While serving the poor of Central America, Danny experienced another miracle in his life. One day, he came across an older man whose face was wrapped in leaves held together by a rag. "What's the matter?" Danny asked. The man could barely speak but managed to explain that his mouth was in great pain. Danny suggested that the poor man visit a dentist. But there was no such medical professional anywhere near this poverty-stricken community.

The only thing Danny could offer was prayer. He laid his hands over the man's head and said: "Jesus, in Your name I ask that You heal this man." The next day the man came running up to Danny, yelling, "You healed me, you healed me." Danny assured the poor man that it was Jesus who had heard his prayers.

After a second tour of duty in the Philippines, Danny was forced to leave the ecumenical missionary organization because he still wanted to be a priest. Danny thought the stage was set. He entered the seminary, thinking that his temporary commitment to celibacy was a natural step to the priesthood. But Danny was about to learn that the call to Holy Orders demands a much deeper discernment. In Danny's mind the only issue he needed to face was whether or not he could honor the Church's celibacy rule. What Danny was about to discover was that the journey to priesthood demands an answer to another question: "Am I called to marry the Church, or is God calling me to marry another?"

Two years later, Danny was offered an opportunity to study in Rome. But before he left to go abroad, he and eleven other seminarians were sent to Mexico to meet Mexican people and learn about their culture. Danny accomplished both objectives when he got to know a lovely young lady by the name of María. Now he had a problem: he loved the Church, and he loved María. He had to make a choice. When he shared the dilemma with his fellow classmates, one of them said: "Just be clear with her." Danny knew that María might be a test. In fairness, he told María that though they might fall in love, he still might choose the priesthood. María was prepared to take that chance.

Over the next few weeks Danny and María spent a great deal of time together, knowing that the decision to become a priest would be made shortly after his upcoming trip to Rome. In that time, the couple talked about what was important to them. Career, family, community, faith, and other "life-changing" topics were thoroughly explored. The chemistry was striking. As Danny said: "We were so similar in our thinking that she could be my wife, my sister, or me." But a promise is a promise. Danny left Mexico to prepare for his trip to study in Rome.

The day Danny came back to the States he went immediately to his spiritual director. At that meeting, the young seminarian announced that he soon would know if he was meant to be a priest or marry María. Much to his surprise, the director said: "You are about to get engaged to the Church. Therefore, you can't go to Rome unless you are prepared to make the choice right now." For Danny, the choice was clear.

After more discernment, it became clear to Danny that he could serve God through marriage. He also realized that his new vocation would not necessarily be the easier road in life. Today, Danny knows he made the right choice, and he and María are expecting their second child.

When asked what words he hopes to hear when he stands before the judgment seat of God, Danny is quick to respond: "Well done, good and faithful servant, for as you have loved María and your children, so too do I love you. Welcome home."

PART II

The Passion

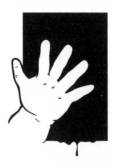

THE AGONY

"He Will Be Called John!"

THESE were the words Saint Elizabeth spoke when the elders asked her to name her newborn son. Her John would later be known as John the Baptist, the same John the Baptist whom Jesus would identify as the one chosen to announce the coming of the Lord! This John was beheaded because he had the courage to stand up to a king and his brother's wife, accusing them of adultery. But the following stories are about other men, all of whom were also named John.

The Apostle John was the younger brother of the Apostle James the Great and the youngest of the twelve to be chosen by Jesus. Barely out of his teens, he would witness the miracles of Jesus, the betrayal by Judas, and the crucifixion of Christ. This apostle would write a Gospel, draft three Epistles, and be credited with writing the Book of Revelation. In addition to his "academic" portfolio, he had a compassionate story to tell.

John was, according to tradition, "the one Jesus loved". He was the same person Jesus took into His confidence regarding which of the apostles would betray the Son of God. As ten of Jesus' closest friends abandoned their Savior, John was the only apostle who had the courage to follow Him on the road to the crucifixion. Jesus appointed John as the protector of His mother, Mary.

What if you could put the following on your resumé: One of only twelve apostles; one of only four Gospel writers; the only apostle who witnessed close at hand the crucifixion of the Son of God; the adopted son of the Mother of God. With all of these credentials, one would think that John would have been readily received by the intellectuals of his time; yet, John and his fellow apostles were described as dangerous rebels and naïve dreamers.

Imagine how this "boy" felt among the men in the group. He had no status. He was the youngest and, by cultural definition, the "least" important. Outsiders might have seen John as a Jesus "groupie", whose value to the group was nothing more than an extra pair of hands.

But John stuck it out. When authorities verbally attacked the Lord, John was at His side. In the garden, where soldiers arrested Jesus, John was prepared to defend his friend. While Jesus was carrying the Cross, being nailed to the Cross, and dying on the Cross, John was but a few feet away. John's fear was overcome by faith; his cowardice by courage; his agony by glory. This is the same John whose name appears at virtually every nationally televised sport-

ing event. Perhaps you have seen his advertisement? John
3:16. His message: "For God so loved the world that He
gave His only Son, so that everyone who believes in Him
might not perish but might have eternal life."

"When Anything Displeasing Happens to You, Remember Christ Crucified, and Be Silent."

These are the words of another John. Born in Spain in
1542, John of the Cross, as he would eventually be known,
was the son of a man who gave up great wealth, status, and
comfort to marry John's mother. His father died when
John was young, forcing his mother and her children to
beg for work. When he was only fourteen, John took a job
caring for patients who suffered from incurable diseases
and madness. It was this experience that taught John to
search for the Cross of Christ where human misery was
present.

John's mother was determined to get her son an education, and eventually the boy was enrolled in a Jesuit
school. Shortly thereafter, the school administrator took a
liking to John and gave his blessing when the young
student announced that he would like to become a priest.
In 1567, John was ordained a priest in the Carmelite
Order. John's passion was about to begin.

At the request of the famous Saint Teresa of Avila,
reformer and foundress of the Discalced Carmelite Order,
John became the spiritual advisor to the sisters, agreeing to
live in a shack that offered nothing more than a place
where John could live in poverty, writing his mystical
poetry and carving crosses. But John's piety and intensity

of prayer got him in trouble with fellow priests, who were threatened by John's insistence on living in the stricter spirit of the primitive rule of the Carmelites. John's adversaries claimed that the "saintly" priest was filled with pride. He was arrested and sent to Toledo, Spain, where he was imprisoned in a six-by-ten-foot cell.

For the next nine months, John was beaten, ridiculed, and forced to live in the sweltering heat and silence of his prison. His "crime" was holiness. It was during this time that John literally lived his "dark night of the soul", an experience whose account would one day be one of the world's most famous mystical writings.

Eventually John escaped the torment of his fellow priests and returned to Avila, where Saint Teresa hid him until he was strong enough to travel. During the next twelve years, John of the Cross continued to encourage Carmelite reforms while setting an example of love for one's enemies and sacrifice for one's God. In 1591, John died after suffering both physically and spiritually at the hands of those in power, who would later be punished for their treatment of this humble priest.

Saint John of the Cross lived his life in the spirit of Jesus' agony in the garden. And because of his sacrifice, one can only envision this same John now tending God's beautiful garden in paradise.

Patron of the Dumb?

Our third "John" comes in the story of a priest who was so academically challenged that he was originally expelled from the seminary, forbidden to hear confessions, and reluctantly sent to the least populated parish in all of France. His name was John Vianney.

As a young boy, John had a special affection for Mary, the Mother of God. In fact he had a favorite statue of the Holy Mother he took to bed each night. When he learned to read, he often would immerse himself in the Gospels. But as for other studies, John struggled at every level of his education including his training as a seminarian. Because his professor was younger and he himself was the oldest student in the class, John quickly became the subject of jokes by fellow classmates. Nevertheless, on August 14, 1815, John was ordained a priest, provided that he would agree not to hear confessions until his understanding of moral theology improved.

As a precaution, church leadership sent the intellectually inept priest to the parish of Ars, which had a total population of 230 people. What this simple assignment needed was precisely a simple-minded priest. Of the fifty families living in the village, only six regularly attended Mass. At his first Mass, Father John Vianney was quite direct as he told the parishioners two things: First, hell exists. Second, it was his job to make sure no one in the village of Ars landed there! From that moment, Sunday crowds began to grow, including men who had frequently used chores as their excuse for not attending Mass. It was not long before Father Vianney received permission to hear confessions. The "grace of God" took over.

This humble priest soon became known for his intense dedication to saving souls. Father Vianney put in twenty-hour workdays saying Mass, hearing confessions, praying privately, teaching the catechism to children, visiting the sick, and saying the rosary. But his hard-hitting sermons

and tireless work were not the only reasons why citizens
from all over France began to come to the village of Ars.
Father John Vianney, a priest originally forbidden to hear
confessions, had another gift: *He could read souls!*

As peasants, noblemen, and fellow priests stepped into
the confessional, they soon learned that nothing could be
hidden from this man. Time and time again, Father
Vianney would stop and challenge the sinner with the
question: "Are you sure there is nothing else you need to
confess?" On one occasion, a woman traveled a great
distance to seek comfort in the mercy of God, hoping her
husband who had committed suicide would be forgiven.
Before she could pour out her grief, Father Vianney
interrupted with the knowledge that her husband had
begged God for forgiveness the moment he leapt from the
bridge; because of that, mercy was his! Frequently, he
would stop hearing the confession of one soul to attend
immediately to the spiritual needs of persons who could
not wait any longer to get an audience with the mystical
priest. Other times, people would try to trick him to prove
that his "gift" was a fraud. They would quickly be ex-
posed. And should a sinner refuse to acknowledge his sins,
Father Vianney would refuse absolution until the truth
came out.

But along with spiritual gifts, as so often is the case,
came spiritual trials. Some priests from other parishes
accused Father Vianney of leading their congregations
away. Many of these same priests warned their parishioners
of how intellectually inept Father Vianney was, not to
mention his unkempt appearance due to inadequate sleep
and the failure to eat regularly. Added to these accusations
was the constant hounding of Satan, who once spoke the

following words through a possessed woman: "If there were three like you on earth, my kingdom would be destroyed. You have taken more than eighty thousand souls from me." Maybe his dent on evil had something to do with the constant rumors that the Blessed Virgin Mary was a frequent visitor to the beleaguered priest.

Eventually the toll of twenty-hour workdays, criticism by fellow priests, attacks by Satan, and the thousands of sins he heard weekly demanded their price. On July 30, 1859, Father John Vianney gave up his soul. And like Joan of Arc, whose death triggered an acknowledgment by an unbeliever that she was a saint, so too did a similar instance occur when the coffin of the famous priest was being carried in the church. At that moment an agnostic cried out: "Truly, this man was a saint."

John the Apostle, John of the Cross, and Father John Vianney had other things in common besides their first name. Each man was ridiculed by some religious authorities and suffered accordingly. Each would be vindicated, as the Gospel of John, the mystical writings of John of the Cross, and the personal inspiration of John Vianney set an example of what it means to practice both compassion and forgiveness. And finally, each "John" offers the young people of this world both courage and conviction as they face their time in the garden.

Gethsemane

Imagine a garden where you go to face the realities of your troubled world, a place where you can begin to search your heart for answers. Your invitation begins with a nagging premonition. Something is not right. You can feel it. It is as if a storm is approaching and you are about to get caught in the downpour. You make believe it is not really happening. Not now. Why me, you ask? It is time to get away. You need a place where you can get the right answers to wrong situations. Maybe you will meet others like yourself. After all, doesn't everyone experience trials and tribulations at one time or another? But this time it is worse than you thought.

The fight with your parents; the failing grade on a critical exam; the betrayal of a friend; the loss of a boy-friend or girlfriend; rejection by the in-crowd; the poor decision to lie, steal, cheat, get drunk, have sex, vandalize another's property, take drugs; the racist remarks; the spreading of pornography; a poor work ethic; the failure to help the poor. These "tears of the soul" are the calling cards needed to enter your garden.

Maybe someone will visit you during your time of sorrow. Someone you can trust. Someone who trusts you and will take your side by acting as a "witness for the defense". After all, it is not your fault. Or is it? Didn't your friends agree when you said, "My parents don't understand me"? Didn't they justify the lie you told your teacher about not feeling well the night before the test? Is it your fault you were misled by others?

Are you kidding yourself? No one will be willing to step forward and take the fall for you. You got yourself into this mess, now it is time to get yourself out. Feel like a leper? Who wants to share in your misery? Who wants to be around someone who has so many problems? Besides, those you wish to invite into your garden are too busy in theirs.

Why is it that the ones who gave you the encouragement are the first to abandon you when you get into trouble? Your parents are idiots, they said. Their advice that you would not get caught echoes in the chambers of your conscience. And as for "those" behaviors, all you wanted was to have some fun. You never meant to hurt anyone. You only meant to have a good time with your friends . . . the friends who no longer want their names mentioned in the same sentence as yours. You are alone in *your* garden.

You argue that it was you who took the risk, but now it is time to face the consequences. Unfortunately, those who sold you out with poor advice often end up cheering as *you* walk to the gallows. How could they act this way? Were not all of you in this together? This was not your private affair, yet it may become your private execution.

Or maybe you feel that what you did was right. Your actions were honorable, you argue. All you did was make a point. Take a stand. Set the tone. Now you find yourself being criticized by the very crowd who supported, even encouraged your actions.

Maybe you should try to undo all you have done. Is

there still time to apologize? Ask for forgiveness? You can explain that you were misunderstood and that everything will be all right now that you have seen the light. Perhaps the time has come for you to deny all you said or did. After all, your friends are worth more than what you stand for, aren't they? It is your choice. Adopt the philosophy that rationalizes that "everyone is doing it." Or enter *your* garden of Gethsemane.

Silent Screams

An anonymous writer once penned some rather simple wisdom. Unfortunately, too many people have missed the point: "When God wants an important thing done in this world or a wrong righted, He goes about it in a very singular way. He doesn't release thunderbolts, or stir up earthquakes. God simply has a tiny baby born, perhaps of a very humble home, perhaps of a very humble mother. And God puts the idea or purpose into the mother's heart. And then she puts it in the baby's mind, and then, God waits. The great events of this world are not battles and elections and earthquakes or thunderbolts. The great events are babies, for each child comes with the message that God is not yet discouraged with humanity, but is still expecting goodwill to become incarnate in each human life."

On January 22, 1973, the Supreme Court issued an order that any woman who wished to destroy the baby in her womb could do so. Those who continue to support the court's ruling have called the decision a victory for the "right to choose". Those who oppose it call the decision what it is: *abortion*! And since that infamous declaration, more than forty million unborn children have been sent to God's garden of sorrows. But along the way there have been "wake-up" calls.

After she aborted her third child, Carol Everett's life began to fall apart. Drinking, an affair, and a broken marriage were all leading to personal destruction. After joining a medical supply company, which eventually led her to the lure of the profit-making abortion industry, she chose to open her own clinic. The money was good, so good that she planned to open four more abortion mills. But that plan got sidetracked when the business consultant she hired turned out to be a preacher. He told her that God had put him in her life that she might turn from this terrible sin. Twenty-seven days later, Carol Everett was no longer in the abortion business. Today, the woman who was once responsible for more than five hundred abortions a month is a nationally recognized speaker whose mission is to expose the lies of abortion.

Another advocate for the abortion industry was a registered nurse by the name of Brenda Pratt Schafer, whose "very" pro-choice position eventually led her to employment at a local abortion mill in Dayton, Ohio. There she witnessed the procedure known as partial-birth abortion. "It was the most horrifying experience of my life", she said. So horrific that she was asked to testify at congressional hearings on the evil occurring in the

Supreme Court-sanctioned industry. Her testimony says it all: "I stood at the doctor's side and watched him perform a partial-birth abortion on a woman who was six months pregnant. The baby's heartbeat was clearly visible on the ultrasound screen. The doctor delivered the baby's body and arms, everything but his little head. The baby's body was moving. His little fingers were clasping together. He was kicking his feet. The doctor took a pair of scissors and inserted them into the back of the baby's head, and the baby's arms jerked out in a flinch, a startled reaction, like a baby does when he thinks that he might fall. Then the doctor opened the scissors up. Then he stuck the high-powered suction tube into the hole and sucked the baby's brains out. Now the baby was completely limp. I never went back to the clinic. But I am still haunted by the face of that little boy. It was the most perfect, angelic face I have ever seen." Brenda Pratt Schafer's experience was her invitation to wake up those who choose to believe that the unborn child is only a blob of tissue designed to interfere with one's life-style.

For Rebecca Wasser, it is quite simple. Life is sacred. Life has purpose. Life is a gift from God. After learning that she was a product of rape, Rebecca began to question if anyone could ever love her. In her mind she was the exception so often quoted in defense of a woman's right to choose. Her birth mother told her that she was conceived through the sin of a serial rapist and that the only reason she was alive today was that a major snowstorm inter-rupted the journey to the abortionist. Her mother also told Rebecca that she loved her.

The reality was a lot to handle for a teenage girl. But for Rebecca, truth became the driving force behind her

desire to succeed in a world that too often justified murder. Motivation led Rebecca to a career in law, advocacy
for the pro-life movement, and a loving family. Rebecca is
a living testimonial to the sanctity of life, as both her
adopted children could themselves, like their adopted
mother, have been candidates for abortion. Her son was
born to a teenage girl who was the victim of date rape.
Her daughter was given up for adoption by an older
woman who candidly admitted, "I made a mistake." For
Rebecca, both her adopted children represent the opportunity to "walk the talk". Today, Rebecca, who was born
on the same day as the decision was made in *Roe v. Wade*
that legalized abortion, encourages teens to read the words
from Psalm 59:1-4: Do not destroy. "Deliver me from my
enemies, O my God, protect me from those who rise up
against me, deliver me from those who work evil, and save
me from bloodthirsty men. For behold, they lie in wait for
my life; fierce men band themselves against me. For no
transgression or sin of mine, O LORD."

Gianna Jessen has a different story to tell. She is a living
abortion. On April 6, 1977, Gianna's biological mother, a
seventeen-year-old who was seven and a half months
pregnant, authorized the injection of a saline solution. But
something happened. Gianna was born before the saline
could take her life. Fortunately, the abortionist, who had
left, did not come back in time to cover up the "botched
abortion". A nurse in the clinic called EMS, who rushed
the two-pound Gianna to the hospital, where she remained for three months. She was diagnosed with cerebral
palsy as a result of the abortion.

When Gianna was nineteen, she was asked to testify
before a House Judiciary Committee. Her words that day

continue to haunt those who try to justify the killing of the unborn. "I am happy to be alive. I almost died. Every day I thank God for life. I do not consider myself a by-product of conception, a clump of tissue, or any other of the titles given to a child in the womb." Gianna went on to say: "I have met other survivors of abortion. They are all thankful for life. Only a few months ago I met another saline abortion survivor. Her name is Sarah. She is two years old. Sarah has cerebral palsy, but her diagnosis is not good. She is blind and has severe seizures. The abortionist, besides injecting the mother with saline, also injects the baby victims. Sarah was injected in the head. I saw the place in her head where this was done. When I speak, I speak not only for myself, but for the other survivors, like Sarah, and also for those who cannot speak."

One who spoke for the unborn was Mother Teresa. In 1979, in Oslo, Norway, she made a critical point in her Nobel Peace Prize acceptance speech. "Abortion . . . is the greatest destroyer of peace today. Because if a mother can kill her own child—what is left for me to kill you and you kill me—there is nothing between." For Gianna, Rebecca, Brenda, Carol, and Sarah, life is everything. They should know. Each has had her time in the garden of Gethsemane. And like their Savior, they were chosen by God to make this a better world.

THE SCOURGING

The Shepherdess

I N 1579, in a small village near Toulouse, France, a young mother in labor waited anxiously for the birth of her child. Moments later, a frail little girl was born with a deformed right hand. Immediately her father was disappointed with his daughter. Her parents gave her the name Germaine. Before the child reached the tender age of three, her mother died. A short time later her father chose to remarry. Germaine's scourging was about to begin.

Germaine's new stepmother was very cruel, isolating the child from her natural children after their birth. In addition to the useless right hand, Germaine had developed seriously swollen glands in her neck that deformed her appearance. This condition was an early form of tuberculosis, common in children who drank milk from infected cows. Germaine's father agreed with the step-mother that such a deformed, infected girl must be kept away from the other children. Germaine's parents and some of the locals considered the young girl to be the village "ugly duckling".

Eventually her banishment meant that she would have to sleep in the stable with the same sheep she tended throughout the day. The only time she was permitted to come to the house was to receive her daily rations of bread. During those times she frequently received beatings from her stepmother.

Fortunately, the time tending sheep allowed her to commune with God and the Blessed Mother as she said the rosary. And though Germaine left her sheep to go to church and receive Holy Communion, not a single one was lost to the bands of roving wolves that frequently attacked unattended animals. On one occasion during a fierce rainstorm, two local villagers testified that a stream actually parted its waters, allowing Germaine to attend Holy Mass.

Germaine's holiness soon caught the eye of the local parish priest, who encouraged her to teach young children about Jesus, His Blessed Mother, and the Catholic faith. Though she never mingled with girls her own age, Germaine was very popular with the children.

As the years passed, Germaine's situation remained the same. At age twenty-two, she could easily pass for a girl of twelve. Her ragged clothes and physical deformities could not hide the spiritual beauty of her soul. It was this beauty that frequently resulted in beatings from her stepmother, who accused Germaine of being evil.

One day, Germaine came across an old man who was begging for food. Racing back to the cottage where she knew her ration of food would be waiting, she quietly slipped into the kitchen and attempted to place her food in her apron. The stepmother caught her and accused the young shepherdess of stealing more than her share of bread. When her stepmother picked up a stick, Germaine ran out of the house with the crazed woman behind her. By the time Germaine reached the village square, she was totally exhausted. Turning to face her stepmother, she unrolled her apron, causing several villagers to gasp, not at the sight of the bread rations, but at the beautiful flowers that were falling to the ground. No one had ever seen flowers of this type anywhere in the region.

From that day forward, Germaine's stepmother, father, and all local villagers had a change of heart toward the outcast. Her parents offered to let her sleep in the house, but Germaine declined, choosing instead to live with the sheep, which had never condemned her. Local children came in great numbers asking Germaine to share her love for God.

One morning the stepmother looked out and noticed that the sheep were still in the stable. Calling out to Germaine, she eventually found that the young girl had died the previous night. The year was 1601.

Forty-three years after her death, two workers lifted the stone covering her corpse only to find Germaine's body had not corrupted. Word spread and crowds of visitors came to see the girl who had once been condemned for her looks. A short time later, miracles of healing began to occur throughout the region.

In 1795, during the French Revolution, an angry

revolutionary destroyed the body. Some fifty-five years later, more than four hundred miracles had been attributed to the young shepherdess. On June 29, 1867, Pope Pius IX declared Germaine a saint.

The story of Saint Germaine in many respects parallels the story of Christ. Jesus was innocent, prayed for His enemies, and accepted the will of God. Germaine, His servant, did the same. Together they shared the scourging.

Dark Night of the Soul

Alone. You know the feeling. Disappointment mounts as parents refuse to listen. All you hear is Mom and Dad making excuses to explain why they do not have time to listen to you. Mom suggests you can come back later. Dad promises that when he gets home he will look you up. Even your brothers and sisters are indifferent. It seems that the entire family has chosen to let you face your problems, your anxieties, your "dark night of the soul" alone.

Later you approach a teacher or coach to see if he will give you some of his time. After listening for a few moments, he too claims it is not really up to him. Sorry, but it is none of his business. You cannot help but think that if the situation were reversed you would be there to help. You do your best to maintain your composure as one adult after another turns his back on you.

Perhaps your close friends will offer to help. Reach out. Listen. But again you are disappointed. The rejection is nauseating. You are beginning to accept the fact that you will have to go it alone. Your dignity is at risk, as everyone seems to wait to see if you are going to break down. You convince yourself it is not the end. You can be strong. You will get out of this fix. It is not over. You will bounce back with, or without, the help of others.

But it seems that every time you attempt to correct the situation nothing works. Conversations do not flow. Explanations do not fly. Friends, family, teachers, coaches, even strangers, all seem to enjoy your internal destruction. Moralizing sermons are all they have to offer. "You should have known better." "What were you thinking?" "How could you?" "What an idiot!" Despair. Revulsion. Disgust. A Greek tragedy in the making. This problem is worse than any scolding you have ever had.

Do they not see that you still have something to offer? You are a good person. You made a mistake. But who among them can claim innocence, you ask. Can they not see that you did your best? Your critics see the situation altogether differently. Accusations, gossip, and backbiting continue, from those you thought cared for you.

Maybe you should remain silent. Perhaps the situation will just blow over. If you try to defend yourself, your so-called friends may choose to crucify you further. If you say you are sorry, will it be enough? It seems that everyone wants you to suffer. You are suffering. Can't they see that? Your conscience confirms the sick feeling in the pit of your stomach. You sense it is time to pay your dues. It is time to face the truth. It is time for your personal scourging.

"By His Wounds, You Have Been Healed"

Remember Saint Francis of Assisi? He was the first person we know of to experience the five wounds of Christ. Punctures in both hands, both feet, and a lance wound in his side spontaneously appeared and were seen as a mystical blessing from God. This event occurred near the end of his life. Almost seven hundred years later, a follower of the teachings of Saint Francis would also experience the stigmata. His name was Padre Pio.

Padre Pio was born in southern Italy in 1887. When he was only fifteen, he began his studies to become a priest, donning the habit of Saint Francis. Seven years later, Padre Pio was ordained in the Order of the Capuchin Friars, pronouncing the vows of poverty, chastity, and obedience.

On September 20, 1918, Padre Pio began to feel pains in his hands and feet. The stigmata had begun. Falling into a deep sleep, the mystic had a vision of Christ crucified. When he awoke, his hands, feet, and side were covered with blood. Though he was in great pain, his only prayer was that the "visible" suffering would be removed so as not to draw attention from the other friars or the outside world. For fifty years, this humble priest suffered the five wounds of Christ. And though he lost about a cup of blood a day, his wounds never became infected.

For Padre Pio, the scourging went far beyond the

stigmata. He suffered violent headaches, experienced gastric problems, faced multiple temptations, was physically attacked by Satan, had a constant fear of damnation, and was accused of being both fraudulent and immoral. Adding to his humiliation, the Pope, acting on information from a jealous archbishop and other priests who suggested that the stigmata was demonic, restricted Padre Pio from saying Mass publicly and from hearing confessions. A weeping Padre Pio would ask: "Why are they doing this to me?" In 1933, all charges were dropped and the archbishop was removed from office.

Returning to his vocation, Padre Pio slept and ate very little as he said daily Mass, heard the confessions of thousands, and welcomed masses of people who came to see the great mystic. His popularity soared as word of miracles and other spiritual happenings began to circulate.

During World War II, an American commander turned his bombers away from a certain Italian village after seeing Padre Pio's image in the sky. On another occasion, Padre Pio invited a physician to touch the wound in his side after the doctor shared a story about a little girl who had a serious illness. The physician later reported that when he touched the little girl with the same hand that had touched the "wound of Christ", the girl was healed. An even more astounding miracle occurred after a grandmother took her blind seven-year-old granddaughter to see the famous priest. After Padre Pio blessed the child, her sight returned. But what makes this miracle all the more chilling is that the little girl's blindness was due to having been born without pupils. After the miracle, the little girl still did not have pupils, yet she could see. Specialists from all over the world have examined the girl only to confirm that there is no way one can see without pupils. In some cases, the doctors were so incredulous that they tried to convince the little girl that she only "thinks she can see"! Such "blindness" is addressed in the second letter of Paul to the Corinthians: "And if our gospel is veiled, it is veiled only to those who are perishing. In their case the god of this world has blinded the minds of the unbelievers, to keep them from seeing the light of the gospel of the glory of Christ, who is the likeness of God" (2 Cor 4:3–4).

Another spiritual gift associated with Padre Pio was his ability to "read" souls. Time and time again, visitors to the confessional reported that their conversations with the mystic focused on the sins of the visitor, not because they confessed their transgressions to Padre Pio, but because he told them what their sins were, when the offense was committed, and with what frequency!

In addition to physical healing and the reading of souls, Padre Pio was seen in two locations at the same time. Stories from soldiers in prison and patients in hospital beds were commonplace, claiming that the priest had administered to their spiritual needs. When his whereabouts at the time of the reported "visitation" were checked, Padre Pio was always in the presence of fellow monastery friars. This "gift" of bilocation was documented in different cities, countries, and continents.

Those who witnessed Padre Pio's stigmata always reported a beautiful smell of violets, roses, or some unearthly odor too pleasant to identify. Ironically, the sense of sight seemed to be distracted from the unpleasant image of bleeding by the sense of smell.

Padre Pio's stigmata disappeared, as he predicted it would, just a few weeks before his death. For fifty years he bore the wounds of Christ. For fifty years he read souls, healed the sick, and converted the lost. During this time the famous priest received more than two million letters from people all over the world. Before he died, he told his fellow friars to destroy all but two. Both letters were written by Cardinal Karol Wojtyla, ten years before he became Pope John Paul II.

In the first letter of Peter 2:24, we read: "He himself bore our sins in his body on the tree, that we might die to sin and live to righteousness. By his wounds you have been healed." Such was the mystery of Padre Pio, a man who lived a life of scourging, so that those he touched might live a life of holiness.

THE CROWNING

"Which Will You Choose?"

THROUGHOUT history, leaders from every continent, country, tribe, and village have made decisions that have far-reaching consequences in the battle of good versus evil. Politicians choose which laws should be written to ensure how parents and their children live their lives. Most lawyers, judges, and Supreme Court justices choose which articles of the Constitution, twenty-six amendments, or other laws and legal decisions should be used to persuade in the court of public opinion. Some physicians choose what is appropriate for you, Mom, Dad, and your grandparents, too often at the expense of those who are unable to defend themselves. Media and entertainment executives choose what you will see, read, hear, wear, or experience, often regardless of the impact it may have on the life God wants you to live. A number of educators will choose which materials you should learn irrespective of the value such content may have in your moral or spiritual development. Certain Wall Street investors choose which stock to buy hoping the transaction will make them money, with little concern about how such decisions will affect your community. Intellectuals choose how and when they should convince young people to buy in to their philosophy, sometimes even if it is in opposition to parents or God. And yet with all the clatter, propaganda, and self-serving prophecies, your generation is mandated to "make the right choice".

The potential danger of the power of persuasion is exemplified by Adolf Hitler. In the early 1930s, Hitler came to power in Germany at a time when there was widespread unrest in the country. Convincing many of the the German people that they were superior to the rest of the world, he proceeded to rally educational, political, and military leadership to join him in the eradication of those citizens who did not meet the qualifications of the "master race". On September 1, 1939, he ordered an attack on Poland. Thus began World War II, which ultimately became the graveyard for more than fifty million people. Six million of those persons were Jewish, most of whom died in the concentration camps.

Two victims of this madness made a choice that for most of us would be out of the question. Edith Stein was born in Poland on October 12, 1891. Though raised as a devout Jew, the highly intelligent daughter of a lumberyard owner renounced her religion at the tender age of thirteen to become an atheist. Some years later she attended the

University of Göttingen, where she became interested in philosophy. Edith Stein graduated *summa cum laude*, earning her doctorate in philosophy.

In 1917, Edith visited Anna Reinach, who was the wife of a favorite professor. Anna was in mourning over the death of her husband, who had been killed in the war. Much to Edith's surprise, the woman she had come to console needed little philosophical comfort. Anna Reinach was a Christian, and her faith was her "rock". This encounter was the turning point for Edith Stein.

Returning to her university, Edith began to learn about Roman Catholicism. She studied the mystical experiences of Saint John of the Cross and the autobiography of Saint Teresa of Avila. Conversion was quick to follow. Though her mother was insistent that her daughter never give up her Jewish faith, Edith was baptized on January 1, 1922. Resigning her college teaching position, Edith chose to teach at a Dominican girls' school. In 1932, she became a lecturer at a German institute but was soon forced to leave because of anti-Semitic legislation passed by the Nazi government.

In 1934, Edith heard the call in her heart to become a nun. She entered the Carmelite convent in Cologne, Germany, and chose the name Teresa Benedicta of the Cross, after her two Catholic role models. In 1938, a decision was made by the Mother Superior of the convent to transfer Sister Benedicta to a convent in the Netherlands, as the threat of Nazi violence against the Jewish people was growing stronger.

Four years later, on July 26, 1942, Adolph Hitler ordered the arrest of all non-Aryan Roman Catholics. With her sister Rosa, also a convert, Edith Stein was arrested by the Gestapo and shipped to the dreaded concentration camp of Auschwitz. Survivors testified that Edith Stein, then known as beloved Sister Benedicta of the Cross, became quickly recognized for her great compassion to those who suffered death camp horrors. On August 9, 1942, Edith Stein, one-time antagonist of God, readily accepted her Lord's will as she was led away to the gas chamber.

Edith Stein once wrote: " 'Thy will be done' must be the rule of Christian life." Those words capture the inspiration of one who chose not to believe in God, who chose to renounce atheism, who chose to become a nun, and who ultimately chose to die for her faith.

As Edith Stein was making her choice, another victim of Hitler's terror was making his. His name was Maximilian Kolbe. Maximilian Kolbe was born on January 7, 1894, in Poland. When Maximilian was a young boy, his mother asked her mischievous son what would become of him. The boy, unsure of the answer, went to the church and knelt down before a statue of the Blessed Mother to see if she had an answer to the question. During his prayer he had a mystical experience in which he saw our Lady standing before him holding two dazzling crowns, one white and the other red. When she asked the boy which one he would choose, he answered, "I choose both." From that moment, Maximilian Kolbe was destined for both purity (white) and martyrdom (red).

Maximilian was incredibly talented in mathematics and physics. He was interested in space flight and actually sketched plans for a spacecraft. But his interest in the stars would have to wait, for he decided to become a Franciscan priest. He was ordained in 1918 and dedicated his life to the Immaculate Heart of Mary. As part of his mission, Maximilian founded the Knights of the Immaculate, whose mission was to work for the salvation of souls, particularly the enemies of the Church.

Father Maximilian Kolbe was stationed in Poland when the Germans invaded. Shortly thereafter, Father Kolbe was arrested and imprisoned in Warsaw, where inflammation of the lungs confined him to a hospital. On May 28, 1941, Father Kolbe and 320 other prisoners were transported to Auschwitz. During that time many of the prisoners asked Father Kolbe to hear their confession. He often led the prisoners in prayer and instructed them to overcome evil by forgiving their persecutors.

One day a prisoner from the cell block housing Father Kolbe escaped. The commandant ordered that ten men be executed in reprisal for the one who got away. All the men were led out to the courtyard, where the commandant arbitrarily selected ten men to die. One of the men, Francis Gajowniczek, cried out for mercy when he learned that he was one of the men chosen. "What will become of my wife and children?" he begged. Suddenly, a prisoner stepped forward and volunteered to take the place of the condemned man. That prisoner was Father Maximilian Kolbe.

Both the commandant and camp guards were stunned at the request. The prisoners themselves were shocked that the SS guards did not shoot the priest who dared to offer a deal for another "worthless" life, not to mention step out of ranks and approach an officer.

Francis, the man whose life was spared, would later write of Father Kolbe: "I observed him evenings in the cell block praying fervently and inviting others to join him . . . a very dangerous activity." Francis goes on to say, "Another day a bunch of us were shoveling manure out of a pit. Father Kolbe was beaten very cruelly by an SS guard, who hit the priest many times in the face while an attack dog also assaulted Father, biting him seriously. Father Kolbe bore all this not just with patience but with dignity. When he returned to the pit where we were throwing out manure, he continued to work without a word."

After Father Kolbe was chosen to die, he was taken to a starvation bunker with nine other men. All of them were stripped and given no food or drink. For days he led the men in prayer by saying the rosary and singing hymns. The guards were again taken aback, for they were used to prisoners screaming from the bunkers. Finally, on August 14, 1941, Father Maximilian Kolbe received his red crown of martyrdom.

Jesus once said that there is no greater love than when one gives up his life for another. Father Kolbe chose to love God by loving his neighbor. It was that decision that earned him and also Edith Stein their "crowns of glory".

"The Choice Is Yours and Yours Alone"

So what is being asked of you? Is it fair to expect that you have the strength to do the kinds of things that saints do? After all, you have been told that if you live a good life heaven will be yours. Is that all it is going to take? Unfortunately, there is something called the "sin of presumption", where one assumes that a ticket to paradise is guaranteed if only you believe in God and the saving grace of Christ. But for Catholics there is the little matter of "doing good works" to go along with one's faith in God. To illustrate, let us imagine that two teenagers are driving around town when suddenly another car runs a light and slams into their car. Both are knocked unconscious. As the ambulance races to the hospital, both teenagers find themselves floating toward what looks like some kind of celestial tunnel. The colors and geometric patterns are stunning, like nothing either teen has ever seen before. There is beautiful music playing, and voices can be heard singing lyrics that only an angel could compose. Speaking of angels, a very large and handsome angel is smiling, ready to greet his guests. Let's listen in on the conversation.

Angel: Welcome, Molly and Brian. I am the Angel Darin. I've been waiting for you.

Molly: Angel! Are we dead?

Brian: D-d-dead?! You must be dreaming, Molly. I mean—hey, wait a minute! This isn't a dream, is it? So, *are* we dead?

Angel: Not yet.

Brian: Wow. Then I guess we'll be leaving for heaven, right?

Angel: Not so fast, Brian, I have a few questions for you first.

Brian: You mean, like a test?

Angel: Sort of. First, Molly. God gave you many gifts. Can you tell me what these are?

Molly: Well, I suppose I have good parents. We live in a nice home, and I attend the best school in the area. Oh, and I have lots of friends, too.

Angel: Molly, I'm more interested about the personal talents God has given you.

Molly: Oh, well, I'm a straight-A student. I'm popular. And I'm a good singer.

Angel: Brian, what about you. What gifts have you been given?

Brian: I get good grades. I'm an all-around athlete. And I'm class president.

Angel: So it sounds as if God blessed both of you with intelligence, leadership, and self-discipline. Is that right?

Molly: I like the way you put that.

Brian: Couldn't have said it better.

Angel: So now that we agree on the gifts both of you have received, could you please tell me how you have shared those gifts with others?

Brian: Well, let me see. Oh, I know! I help my younger brother with his algebra. As for sports, my teammates rely on my batting and pitching to win games. And I work with the school administration to point out what is needed to improve student–teacher relationships.

Angel: Molly, what about your contributions?

Molly: Because I'm one of the best singers in the school, I always participate in school plays. When asked, I help other students who need assistance in their homework. And, because I'm popular I can be a role model to others.

Angel: Does either of you know the meaning of "proper pride"?

Molly: I thought pride was a sin.

Brian: I heard that too. But then, shouldn't you be proud of your achievements?

Angel: Yes, on both counts. But proper pride means "To multiply in the lives of others those talents one receives from God." So for Molly, being popular is not simply being available if and when someone needs a role model. It means setting an example by the way she thinks, speaks, and acts twenty-four hours a day, seven days a week, regardless of whom she is with or for what purpose. Said another way: It is "servant leadership".

Angel: Brian, you said that the team relies on you both to hit and to pitch well.

Brian: That's right.

Angel: Well, using your baseball analogy, a servant leader knows when and how to demonstrate good sportsmanship, help and encourage less-gifted athletes, and handle defeat with dignity.

Molly: I didn't say I wanted to be a leader.

Angel: No. But you did agree that both you and Brian have been blessed with intelligence, self-discipline, and leadership capabilities. As such, both of you are smart enough to know when others need your help. Both of you have the work ethic needed to set an example. And each of you recognizes that you have the potential to influence friend and stranger alike.

Brian: I don't know about my "servant leadership" potential; all I know is that I want to get into heaven and to do that I need to know what God expects of me.

Angel: First, God wants you to love Him by "living" the Ten Commandments. Second, He wants you to love your neighbor. One way to do the latter is to multiply in the lives of others those talents you have been blessed with.

Molly: Oh, the "proper pride" thing.

Angel: Right. And if you follow this advice, you will learn to discern right from wrong; have the conviction to stand up for what you believe in; forgive your enemies; reach out to the less fortunate by offering time, talent, or money; be faithful in your obligations; and practice self-control in both behavior and life-style.

Molly: And if we do, what then?

Brian: Yes, what happens next?

Angel: What happens next is that both of you are about to regain consciousness. After that it is up to you. You can choose good or you can choose evil. You can choose to be a servant leader, or you can choose to be led. Whichever you do, the choice is yours, and yours alone.

Against All Odds

At the beginning of this chapter, we were introduced to two "saints of God" whose courage and compassion earned them the crown of martyrdom. What follows are the stories of two men who, like Maximilian Kolbe and Edith Stein, were faced with the evils of the Nazi regime. But unlike Kolbe and Stein, who died for their faith, these men survived because of theirs.

Monsignor Hugh O'Flaherty was assigned to the Vatican during World War II. Because of the Vatican's neutrality, there was an understanding that German occupying forces would not take over the Catholic Church's holy capital. But Father O'Flaherty was not about to let evil stand in the way of his duty as a priest. Using his influence among Roman and Italian leaders, the monsignor smuggled refugees into the city of Rome, hiding many Jewish families in various convents and apartments. In the spring of 1943, his operation broadened to include escaped British prisoners of war. In September of that year, the German Gestapo occupied the city. The Nazi Gestapo leader, Colonel Kappler, made it clear to Church hierarchy that any religious who attempted to hide Jews or other enemies of the "fatherland" would be shot.

In the months to come, Colonel Kappler was increasingly suspicious of the monsignor's role, suspecting the priest had something to do with the smuggling of Jews. Yet every evening Father O'Flaherty would meet his contacts outside the Vatican and coordinate an elaborate underground network of safe houses. Many times the priest would dress up as a nun, beggar, or Swiss Guard to avoid capture.

One day the German ambassador told Father O'Flaherty, "Nobody in Rome honors you more than I do for what you are doing. But it has gone too far for all of us. If you ever step outside the Vatican walls again you will be arrested at once. Now please think about what I have said!" The monsignor politely replied, "I will certainly think about what you have said, sometimes."

The courage of Monsignor O'Flaherty and others in and outside the Vatican resulted in the saving of more than 8,700 Jews, many of whom were secret occupants of O'Flaherty's residences. One person who was saved by the mercy of Father O'Flaherty was not a Jew. He was Colonel Kappler, the same Gestapo henchman who did everything he could to try to catch and ultimately execute the priest. Captured by the Allies, Colonel Kappler was imprisoned near Rome. For many years after the war, the prisoner had only one visitor. His name was Monsignor Hugh O'Flaherty. In 1959, Colonel Kappler was baptized into the Catholic Church by a former enemy.

Our second story involves another soldier. But unlike Edith Stein and Father Maximilian Kolbe, who died at the hands of the dreaded German SS, Gereon Goldmann was in fact a member of that same SS unit responsible for the deaths of thousands of innocent victims all over Europe.

Before Gereon Goldmann earned the SS designation, he was a first-year seminary student seeking to wear the habit of the Franciscans. Unfortunately, he was drafted into the German army at the start of World War II and eventually transferred into the special Nazi unit.

A few days before he was to leave for the Russian front, he returned to his hometown, where he happened to stop and pray at the local church where he had once served as an altar boy. As he stood to go, an elderly nun approached and asked if he remembered her. He did and was surprised that she remembered him. "I should", she said. "I've been praying for you, that one day you would become a priest."

Goldmann stated that he hoped to finish his studies after the war. At that, the kindly sister said, "That day has come. This year you will be ordained." Goldmann laughed and assured the nun that his ordination would be quite impossible as he would be leaving for Russia the next day. Though the sister insisted her prophecy would come to pass, nothing could convince the young SS soldier. As he was boarding the train, Gereon Goldmann heard her say that the Blessed Mother would play a part in answering her prayers. Goldmann smiled and sat back as the train left the station.

The next day, back at camp, hundreds of German soldiers were ready to leave for their trip to the Russian front. At the moment Gereon Goldmann was about to board the train, he heard his name being paged. Moments later, he learned that his orders had been changed and that he would be going to France to be stationed near a small town by the name of Lourdes, the same village where our Lady had appeared to Bernadette Soubirous. This was the first of many miracles to happen to Gereon Goldmann.

In the next few years, the man who wore the dreaded SS uniform escaped death when nearly everyone around him was killed, was ordained by permission of the Pope even though he had only one year of seminarian schooling, managed to convert the most hardened Nazis captives while in a prisoner-of-war camp, and was saved from execution through the intervention of a number of French nuns and priests.

God had other plans for Gereon Goldmann, just as He did for Hugh O'Flaherty, Edith Stein, and Maximilian Kolbe. All four experienced the horrors of war. All four trusted in God and His divine providence. And all four chose the crown of glory.

THE CROSS

"And upon This Rock"

His name was Simon. He was a fisherman. He was uneducated. He was poor. But one day, while fishing with his brother Andrew, he received a rather unusual invitation from a stranger. "Come after Me, and I will make you fishers of men." At those words, Simon, who would be renamed Peter (meaning "rock"), would follow Jesus to the "cross". Peter's journey would be one demanding courage, conviction, and humility. And because he was all too human, Peter would suffer many failures. But he was the "rock", and upon this rock, Christ would build His Church.

Imagine for a moment what you would do if you were approached by a charismatic speaker whose words stimulated massive followings of young people and adults. Now imagine that this person could heal the sick, make the blind see, raise the dead, and feed five thousand people with only five loaves and two fish. And what if this person had a unique way of shaming those whose arrogance demanded rebuke, while at the same time loving those whom no one dared love. Do you think you might end up following him wherever he went? Do you think that you might want to emulate his example? Do you think that if he offered you a job to be his Chief Operating Officer you would accept? Peter did. And during those three years he spent with the Son of God, he could have been fired on at least three occasions. Instead, Peter was given the glory of the cross.

Peter had witnessed hundreds of miracles, one of the first being for his own mother-in-law, who was very sick. When the Lord placed a hand on her forehead, the fever left her. On another occasion, Peter was in a boat with Jesus and the rest of the disciples when a sudden storm came up. The apostles were convinced they were going to drown. Crying out to Jesus, they pleaded: "Teacher, do you not care that we are perishing?" Jesus got up, calmed the storm, and said: "Why are you terrified? Do you not yet have faith?" This question of faith would surface later for Peter when once again he was sailing with the rest of the disciples. This time, Jesus was not present. Looking out on the water, the fishermen suddenly saw Jesus walking toward them and feared it was a ghost. Jesus called out, "Take courage, it is I; do not be afraid." Peter spoke up, saying, "Lord if it is you, command me to come to you on the water." Jesus motioned to Peter, and the Apostle began to walk on the water toward the Lord. But when Peter realized what he was doing, his fear overcame him and he began to sink. At that moment he cried out, "Lord, save me!" Jesus reached out his hand and saved Peter from drowning. "O you of little faith, why did you doubt?" Jesus asked. This incident would not be the last time Peter's faith would be at issue.

A short time later, in a private conversation with the apostles, Jesus made His first prediction that He would be crucified. Peter immediately disagreed with the Lord, saying that no such thing would ever happen. At that, Jesus said to His hand-picked leader, "Get behind me, Satan! You are an obstacle to me. You are thinking not as God does, but as human beings do." In most scenarios, once you contradict the CEO, you are fired! But in Peter's case, the Lord understood the weakness inherent in this apostle.

Peter dared to disagree with Jesus another time, when the Lord, according to Jewish custom, started to wash the feet of all the apostles before the Passover meal. "You will never wash my feet", Peter boldly declared. Jesus answered, "Unless I wash you, you will have no inheritance with me." Again, Peter was put in his place. And if this were not enough, the Lord again got Peter's attention when the Apostle proclaimed, "I will lay down my life for you." At this statement, Jesus startled Peter and all the apostles with these words: "Will you lay down your life for me? Amen, amen, I say to you, the cock will not crow before you deny me three times."

Before the denials occurred, Peter made an attempt to defend his Lord when the chief priests and Pharisees tried to arrest Jesus in the garden of Gethsemane. After striking off the ear of one of the slaves about to apprehend Jesus, Peter was ordered to put away his sword and let prophecy be fulfilled. Hours later, Peter, as Christ had predicted, denied he even knew Jesus. First, there was the maid in the courtyard who spoke up. "You too were with Jesus the Galilean", she said. Then there was the girl outside the gate, who yelled, "This man was with Jesus the Nazorean." Finally, there was the slave who came over to Peter sitting by the fire. "Didn't I see you in the garden with him?" he asked. Enough was enough. Peter began to curse, "I do not know the man." At that moment, Peter heard the cock crow. And then he remembered Jesus' words: "Before the cock crows you will deny me three times." Peter ran away, weeping bitterly.

Peter had seen Jesus heal lepers. He had been present when Jesus drove evil spirits out of possessed men. He had seen his Master straighten a man's withered hand. He had witnessed the dumbfounded looks on the faces of sinners when they realized their souls had just been read, and he had seen the same startled look on intellectuals who dared to try to trap the Son of God. And though Peter had experienced what the prophets foretold, "the rock" ran away.

But Peter would experience his own resurrection. He would lead the apostles in their evangelization efforts, heal the sick, raise the dead, and set the standard for all future Popes. And when Peter learned that he was going to be crucified, tradition has it he requested that his body hang upside down, for, as he told his executioners, he was not worthy to die the same way his Savior had.

Courage. Conviction. Humility. These traits earned Peter the right to carry the cross. And two thousand years later, the Church stands, and the gates of hell have not prevailed against her.

Your Way of the Cross

There will be times when you are asked to carry the "cross". There will be times when you are called upon to recognize the "cross" others carry. And there will be times when others will ask if you could help carry their "cross". In all cases, when you say Yes to the way of the cross, you are saying Yes to the Savior who carried His Cross for you.

Let's look at the first situation. When Mom or Dad asks you to give up some time in order to help them with chores, you have two choices. You can complain, or you can offer up your sacrifice to God. The same goes when you are asked to volunteer or give a donation or help someone in school whom you do not really know. Accept the annoying habits of your siblings, attend a boring family affair, or even sit through a dull lecture. Why not wear clothes only your parents like, or eat the food that is put in front of you, regardless of what it tastes like? Spend time with relatives you really do not like. In all cases, you have been invited to make a simple sacrifice. Is it really too much to ask?

Most assuredly, there will be more difficult "crosses" you will have to carry. If a parent gets sick, loses a job, or dies, you will better understand what suffering is all about. Sooner or later you will experience a setback in some academic, athletic, or social endeavor. As you enter the world of work, a new set of challenges will surface.

Marginal pay, menial tasks, difficult people, and inflexible schedules will test your fortitude. Then there is marriage. Suddenly, you will recall the phrase "for better or worse". Soon thereafter, God may bless you and your spouse with children. And if He does, you will be expected to handle the crying infant, the "terrible twos", the even more "terrible teens", and the loss of your child to a sweetheart, college, or a job transfer. Maybe you will suffer from an acute illness, lose your ability to get around, or find out that you have only so much time left on this earth. For some, the "cross" of despair is in their future.

Even now you may be asked to carry a cross that goes with being unpopular, less than beautiful, overweight, academically challenged, or a poor athlete. Perhaps your cross has to do with your family. Your dad is an alcoholic. Your mother is horribly obese. Your sister is carrying a married man's child. Your brother is in jail.

Maybe the burden you carry has more to do with image. It starts with the address on your mailbox. Your family is poor. The car in your driveway is old and won't start. The clothes you wear stand out, not because you are up on the latest fashions, but because the styles you wear are what your parents wore when they were in school. Not only do you have trouble finding your way to the game, or having some decent clothes to wear, but you cannot even pay for your meal at the restaurant.

Whatever the circumstances, there will be many opportunities to offer up your "cross" to Christ. Should you make this choice, others will learn from your example. Teach them to be strong. Teach them to pray for the "grace" to accept their station in life. Teach them that there will always be others who need their help. Teach them to give thanks to God for what they do have, while asking Him to show them what they can do for Him. If you accept this calling, you will soon observe others following your "way of the cross".

Walk a Mile in Their Shoes

Ever wonder why certain people act the way they do? You know the type. They are distant, unfriendly, even threatening. Others say that they cannot be trusted. You have heard that their family is "weird". They never seem to smile, never want to get involved. Perhaps their style of dress does not measure up. Whatever it is, they just do not fit in. "Whatever it is . . ." The words should provide a reality check, for they may indicate that you really do not know this person. You have never met his family. And why she never seems to smile may have something to do with the fact that she has nothing to smile about. Ever think about that?

What if your parents were fighting the night before? Do you think you would be in a cheery mood the next day? If you were new at school and none of the students warmed up to you, how would you react? If you just found out that your mom was diagnosed with breast cancer, would you care what others thought about your sadness? What if you lost your schoolbooks, damaged your dad's car, got a bad grade, lost a friend, did not make the team, or were fired. In that moment, would you really be concerned what others said about your indifference to their socialization needs? I don't think so.

We too often have no idea why some people act the

way they do. All we care about is our feelings. It does not matter to us if the estranged person is having personal problems. All that is important is for us not to have to participate in their misery. In fact, sometimes we are so caught up in our world, we do not realize that our personal selfishness may be the number one reason why we are the recipients of their unhappiness. "We reap what we sow."

So the next time someone is unresponsive to our expectations, instead of condemning him, we should be ready to listen, help, forgive, pray. Because for all we know, God has put this person in our life to help us understand that there will be times when our only job is to recognize that others have a "cross" to carry. If you take this step, you are well on your way to living the words of Christ: "This is my commandment, that you love one another as I have loved you" (Jn 15:12).

"He Ain't Heavy, He's My Brother"

In the Gospel narrative, Luke writes: "And as they led him away, they seized one Simon of Cyrene, who was coming in from the country, and laid on him the cross, to carry it behind Jesus" (Lk 23:26). This stranger is known some two thousand years later as Blessed Simon. Circumstances suggest that Simon's act of charity was not voluntary. In all likelihood, he was forced by Roman soldiers to help a condemned man. But forced or not, he is remembered because he did an act of kindness for another.

How many times in your life have you been asked to help others? It is easy to come to the aid of your best friends. Surely, they would do the same for you. And most of the time it is easy to give your mom or dad a helping hand. After all, they are your parents. If favorite teachers or coaches ask for a favor, the likelihood that you would reject their request is "slim and none". But the test of kindness is when the stranger helps the stranger, the enemy helps the enemy, or the popular helps the unpopular.

To help others carry their cross is Servant Leadership. To reach out to those in need is to emulate Christ. To sacrifice your time, money, talent, or pride is to "love thy neighbor". The wisdom of Saint Peter in his first letter to the Christian communities makes the point when he says: "Above all, hold unfailing your love for one another, since love covers a multitude of sins" (1 Pet 4:8).

Reaching out to those in need can be as dramatic as sacrificing a kidney to save another's life or as simple as helping a fellow student better understand a mathematical formula. In both cases, you are helping someone carry a cross. And should you choose to help the stranger, the enemy, or the one who has no friends, your act of charity will bring even greater favor at the judgment seat of God. Remember what Jesus said: "For if you love those who love you, what reward have you? . . . And if you salute only your brethren, what more are you doing than others?" (Mt 5:46–47).

What Jesus challenges us to do is to show charity to all, regardless of our affiliation with them. To do so, seek out the obvious. Help those who hunger for a meal. Give your time to the lonely. Listen to those who need to talk to someone. Invite the outsider to participate in your social gatherings. Share your gifts with the less gifted. Forgive him whose intrusion in your life is nothing more than a plea for friendship. Show patience with those who need understanding. Forgive those who need your forgiveness. Be tolerant, respecting different races, religions, cultures, and customs. Stand up for the weak, demanding equal treatment for all, in educational, economic, and vocational arenas.

In short, become the "Blessed Simon" to those who need help in carrying their crosses. Jesus said: "As you did it to the least of these my brethren, you did it to me." And because you loved your neighbor, the Lord will be there to help you carry your cross.

"Be Not Afraid!"

On October 16, 1978, Karol Wojtyla (pronounced Voi Tee Wa) began his reign with the words, "Be not afraid." With this decree, the world was introduced to Pope John Paul II, the 264th Bishop of Rome. The story of this remarkable man is the story of the "cross".

Born in Poland on May 18, 1920, Karol Wojtyla was the youngest of three children. His sister died in infancy, his mother when he was but eight years old, and his older brother three years later. The last of his family, his beloved father, died in 1941. As Pope John Paul II would later remark, "At twenty I had already lost all the people I loved and even those I might have loved, like my older sister who, they said, died six years before I was born."

Added to his sorrow was the loss of many friends who were murdered in Auschwitz, a Nazi death camp. His Polish culture was nearly destroyed as professors were executed, Jews murdered, families broken, and religion oppressed. But Wojtyla, having received a model upbringing from a father who treasured his faith, put his trust in the Sacred Heart of Jesus and the Immaculate Heart of Mary. In 1943, Karol Wojtyla joined a youth group dedicated to the rosary. These young men were committed to prayer and support of their fellow brothers, all of whom were under suspicion by the Nazi Gestapo.

This trust in God led Karol to the priesthood, where he was ordained in November 1946, after secretly attending an underground seminary. During those "dark years", six million of his countrymen died. Though the war was technically over, Poland would again be occupied, this time by the atheistic Soviet Union. Priests disappeared, Jews were murdered, and the general populace was enslaved.

But Karol Wojtyla would not let evil disrupt his service to the Church. At age thirty-eight he was made the youngest bishop in Poland. Six years later he was appointed archbishop, and only three years after that, Pope Paul VI made the forty-seven-year-old priest a cardinal of the Church.

His reputation spread beyond communist Poland, as his engaging style, mastery of multiple languages, and outreach to people of all persuasions quickly earned him the respect of Catholics and non-Catholics worldwide. On October 16, 1978, after the sudden death of John Paul I, Karol Wojtyla was elected Pope at age fifty-eight. Thus began the pontificate of John Paul II.

Whether speaking to cardinals or priests, presidents or peasants, parents or children, his message was the same: "Be not afraid!" Time and time again, Pope John Paul II would practice what he preached. Though one of the world's most powerful men, he took the time to walk the streets of Italy to chat with the common people, blessing their children, marrying their daughters, or ordaining their sons. When he returned for a visit to his beloved Poland and challenged the Soviet authorities, he stood firm as more than one-third of the entire country came out to cheer their native son. When a would-be assassin shot him, he trusted in the protection of the Blessed Mother that he would survive. When the media and many Americans said that the youth in this country were too distracted by sex, drugs, and a materialistic society, he ignored their advice and reached out to the largest crowd of young people ever to descend upon Denver, Colorado. He did the same in Morocco before eighty thousand young Muslim citizens. Regardless of threats on his life, he addressed more than five million people in the Philippines in a single World Youth Day event in Manila. When he knew he would be ridiculed for his stands on abortion, euthanasia, capital punishment, married priests, women's rights, population control, and the "culture of death", he stood his ground, defending the sanctity of life and the teachings of the Church. Though he fell and broke a hip, slipped and broke his shoulder, and had surgery for a tumor, he was not afraid.

After Karol Wojtyla honored his fellow cardinals' request that he become the next Pope, he realized he would read the Third Secret of Fatima. When the Blessed Mother appeared to three children in 1917, she gave three predictions, two of which were shared with the world. The first was that World War I would soon end, but a more terrible war would follow if the human race did not turn from sin. Our Lady told the children that a mysterious sign would appear in the sky foretelling the advent of a second world war. On the evening of January 25, 1938, an unusual display of northern lights lit up the European sky. Thirty days later Hitler marched into Austria. Eighteen months later, Poland was invaded and World War II was under way.

The second prediction told of the evils of Russia and how the errors of communism would spread throughout the world unless that country and its people were converted and consecrated to Mary's Immaculate Heart.

The third prediction, until recently, was not shared with the world. Almost the only people who had read the message were John XXIII and succeeding Popes. For more than twenty years, John Paul II had lived with the knowledge that he might be the Pope destined to fulfill the secret. On May 13, 1981, sixty-four years to the day after the first apparition of the Blessed Mother to the children of Fatima, the Bishop of Rome had lain seriously wounded from a gunshot wound he received while circling Saint Peter's Square. Pope John Paul II had reason to believe he would live. In the summer of 2000, Pope John Paul II announced that the Third Secret of Fatima had predicted that a future Pope would survive an attempted assassination.

Another prediction about this Pope was recorded in a diary written by the Polish mystic Sister Faustina. Writing in 1938, eight years before Karol Wojtyla was ordained a priest, this sister, a member of Cracow's Sisters of Our Lady of Mercy Congregation, wrote that as she was praying for Poland she heard the voice of Jesus, who said: "I bear a special love for Poland, and if she will be obedient to My will, I will exalt her in might and holiness. From her will come forth the spark that will prepare the world for my final coming."

The Pope who has carried the "Cross of Christ" to every continent on the globe has given each young person two reasons to hope, Jesus and His Blessed Mother. And that optimism is contained in three little words: "Be Not Afraid!"

THE CRUCIFIXION

Golgotha

OUTSIDE ancient Jerusalem there was a hill that was called Golgotha. And it was in this place that Jesus was crucified almost two thousand years ago. Our name for this place, Calvary, is from *Calvaria*, the Latin translation of the Aramaic *Golgotha*, or the place of the skull. There is no record of how many people met their deaths on this spot. But we do know about some of the saints who, in the name of Christ, chose to endure a painful death, a personal crucifixion in lands far from the shores of Palestine. Three such men were Isaac Jogues, John Gabriel Perboyre, and Charles Lwanga.

Isaac Jogues was born in 1607, in France. After joining the Jesuits, Father Jogues traveled to North America to bring Christianity to the Indian tribes in southern Canada. One tribe that accepted Father Jogues and his companions was the Hurons.

One day while sailing down a river with Huron Indians, Father Jogues and his assistant René Goupil and their party were attacked by a large band of Iroquois braves. The attackers viciously killed many Hurons while capturing others and the Jesuits who were with them. The prisoners were taken to villages where horrible tortures awaited them. Over the next sixteen months Father Jogues witnessed a number of captives being burned alive. Others were made to run the gauntlet while Iroquois braves maimed their victims with clubs. Even Iroquois children got in the act as they frequently threw hot coals on the bare backs of captives. Father Jogues was not spared, as he personally suffered both physical and personal pain. René Goupil had his head split wide open with a tomahawk and his body dragged around the village for all to see.

Regardless of the horrors, Father Jogues continued to pray for the conversion of his enemies while secretly baptizing many of their children. He also took care of several Iroquois braves who became sick. Many of these Indians were the same ones who had inflicted some of the worst tortures on Father Jogues and his fellow captives.

Eventually Father Jogues escaped and boarded a ship for France, arriving on Christmas morning 1643. After his arrival, Father Jogues was in great demand to speak before both Church and French leaders about the harrowing trials he had undergone. In a letter dated August 5, 1643, that was delivered to the French Jesuit Provincial, Father Jogues vividly described his hour of crucifixion:

They turned on me with their fists and knotted sticks, left me half-dead on the ground, and a little later tore away my nails in the same way, and bit off my two forefingers which caused me incredible agony. They did likewise to René Goupil. . . . They wanted however to take me into their country alive. So moved by cruel mercy, they carried me covered in blood from wounds, especially in the face, to a hill on which they erected a stage. They now loaded me with a thousand insults and dealt me fresh blows on neck and body. They burned one of my fingers, crushed another under their teeth, and so twisted the bruised and torn sinews of the remainder, that although at present partially healed, they are crippled and deformed.

Despite all Father Jogues had lived through, he asked to be sent back to Montreal, where he hoped to effect a peace between the Iroquois and other tribes in French Canada. Promised by the Iroquois leadership that the Jesuit priest would be welcomed among the people, Father Jogues ventured back to the very tribe that had mutilated his hands and murdered his friends. On October 18, 1644, Father Isaac Jogues met his final crucifixion when he was tomahawked and then decapitated. One can only wonder how many Iroquois babies he had baptized and children he had taught may have surrounded him as he walked through the gates of heaven.

In 1835, another French priest, Father John Gabriel Perboyre, was about to leave for China. He knew of the impending danger, as missionaries were often persecuted for preaching Christianity. After working among the people for four years, Father Perboyre was finally arrested. He experienced more than forty interrogations. Though he was beaten across the face with bamboo rods, forced to kneel on broken glass, and made to drink the boiling blood of a dog, Father Perboyre refused to trample the crucifix. Accused of hiding other Christian "criminals", Father John Gabriel Perboyre was sentenced to death. With no malice toward his perpetrators, this gentle priest was prepared to die for his faith.

On September 11, 1840, the executioners tied Father Perboyre's arms to a low cross, placed a cord around his neck and slowly but painfully strangled the man of God. It was reported from several Christians and pagans alike, that as the priest was dying, the sign of the cross appeared in the sky. He was only thirty-eight years old when he suffered his crucifixion.

Charles Lwanga, like John Gabriel Perboyre and Isaac Jogues, was martyred for his faith. But unlike the French priests who died at the hands of people in foreign lands, Charles Lwanga was murdered by his own people in May 1886, in Uganda, Central Africa.

Charles Lwanga was one of the most popular men in the king's court and was influenced by Joseph Mukasa, the chief steward over the king's pages. Charles' respect for Joseph grew when he witnessed Joseph condemn the king for murdering a Protestant missionary. Such courage cost Joseph his life, and on November 15, 1885, he was beheaded and then burned. After this event, Charles Lwanga was assigned the responsibility for the royal pages. Like Joseph before him, Charles had a strong influence over Uganda's young men, many of whom would follow Charles' example from baptism through death.

His journey to martyrdom began when one of the servant boys was called to the king's quarters to satisfy the ruler's pedophilia. When the boy did not show up, the king learned that an aide to his court had been teaching the youngster about the Catholic faith. Flying into a rage, the king executed the young man's instructor. He then ordered all Christians to be delivered before the royal court, where he ordered: "Those who do not pray stand by me, those who do pray stand over there."

Charles Lwanga gathered all the Christians and prayed with them that they might be strong in their faith. When the king asked Charles and the others if they were prepared to die for their faith, all stepped forward professing their love for Jesus Christ. Even one of the king's bodyguards joined the Christian prisoners.

All told, twenty-two Christians would face unbelievable tortures. After a thirty-seven-mile death march, a number of the Christians were beaten to death. Others had their limbs and heads cut off. Some were burned alive. When Charles offered to help build the pyre of wood necessary to burn his body, the executioners could only marvel. As Charles was dying, he was overheard to cry out, "*Katonda*! (O my God!)"

The death of Saint Charles Lwanga and his twenty-one friends was the seed needed to spread Christianity throughout the land. Today, there are more than two million Christians in Uganda.

"Eloi, Eloi, Lama Sabachthani?"

"My God, my God, why have You forsaken me?" Have you heard those words before? Have you cried those words yourself? Haven't we all? Those were the words Jesus spoke moments before He died on the Cross. At first blush it seems that there is a contradiction, as the saints who gave their lives for their faith did so in eager anticipation to join their Savior in paradise, yet the same Christ whose name they whispered at the moment of their death appears to suggest that He had been abandoned at the moment of His death. In reality, Jesus was fulfilling King David's prophecy centuries before the birth of Christ. David's message, recorded in the twenty-second Psalm, is recognized as "the prayer of an innocent person". As Jesus was dying on the Cross, He cried out to the Father, for the Father is the only One who will answer the prayer of the Son.

Remember this the next time you feel a crucifixion coming on. You know what it is like. You cannot concentrate. You suffer in silence. The headache begins. The pit in your stomach tells you that stress is eating away at your soul. You cannot sleep. You have lost your appetite. Everything seems confusing as you try to make the most of your situation. You ask: Why is this happening? Why do I have to be the victim? What price am I going to have to pay, and is it worth it? And then you remember.

Molly is hurting because her brother has dropped out

of school, causing incredible tension in the family. Brandon just found out that his dad has cancer. His father has only a few months to live. A favorite coach just learned that his mom died of a heart attack. Donny, one of the best players on the baseball team, has quit since he learned that his parents are getting a divorce. The pressure is too much. Terri Lynn, the new girl in school, continues to miss classes as she cares for a dying mother. Justin, the smartest student in the junior class, was just arrested for selling drugs. He had so much going for him. One of the girls in your class was raped, while another has to deal with an alcoholic father. And the boy too often the target of cruel jokes was just told by the doctors that he has been diagnosed with Tourette's syndrome. Now you understand why his behavior was so odd.

The list goes beyond students, friends, and teammates. The neighbor just lost his job after twenty-five years working for the same company. Television newscasters report yet another tragedy involving a local child. The mailman delivers a request for financial aid. If the offer is ignored, another homeless person will go hungry, the letter says. And your parents continue to talk about their friends' children, who seem to be in worse shape than you.

You are not alone. There are others who have similar problems. Then there are those whose problems make yours look like a broken fingernail. You are not alone. There are parents, teachers, coaches, counselors, and other adults who will reach out to you if you give them the chance. The same can be said for those friends who truly care what happens to you. You are not alone. When you feel as if the weight of the world is on your shoulders, think of Him who died for the sins of that same world. For

God the Father has given you the gift of His Son. Jesus is the spiritual foundation necessary to receive the grace needed to get you through your time of trial. He has promised that you will not be tested beyond what you can handle. In fact, He may allow you to be tested so you will learn what you can handle.

To help you pass the test, consider the following: First, you need to pray. Ask Jesus and His Blessed Mother to help you as you face difficulties in your life. Second, you need to strengthen your spiritual portfolio. Read the Holy Scriptures, attend Mass, receive the sacraments, and pray the rosary. Third, you need to offer up your sufferings for others in union with Christ, as did those who died for their faith. And fourth, you need to realize that throughout your life trials will surface. Whether you are in high school or college, have a professional or family life, have children or grandchildren, the time to invite God into your life is not reserved for times of trouble.

Even in your darkest hour, God will never abandon you. Be sure you never abandon Him.

The Man Who Forgave God

Larry Vuillemin had it all. Outstanding athlete, personality, good looks, good grades, and a loving family were factors in his being chosen as "the most likely to succeed". Raised by parents who loved their Catholic faith, it was not unusual for Mom and Dad to have their daughter and five sons join in the rosary while traveling to destinations of fifteen minutes or more. Mom had a special devotion to the Blessed Mother; Dad was an usher at Sunday Mass. Together, they set an example for their children in how to "live" one's faith.

One day, Larry's perfect world was shattered. His greatest cheerleader, his Dad, dropped dead of a heart attack at age forty-eight. The family was devastated. How could God do this to a man who had faithfully attended daily Mass and raised his children in the Catholic faith and who was a loving husband of a God-fearing woman? Larry recalls: "We buried Dad twice, once in the ground, the other in our hearts." Larry believed that a young man must be courageous and never grieve publicly, much less cry out to God. Such behavior would be a sign of weakness.

Larry's star continued to rise as he made the Ohio all-state football team, following in the steps of his older brother, who now played for Notre Dame. And like his "role model" brother, Larry later attended Notre Dame on a full scholarship. In his junior year he met his future wife, and they were married one year later. During these years, God was not invited to be part of Larry's life.

In 1970, Larry graduated from Notre Dame. But his joy was short-lived, as he and his family learned that the brother who had just signed a contract with the Washington Redskins was now in a New York hospital suffering from schizophrenia, a psychotic disorder characterized by withdrawal from reality. Larry's brother would never play football again. As for Larry, he thought another one of his heroes had been struck down by God.

Larry continued his education, and, like his father, he became a prosecuting attorney. Having graduated valedictorian, Larry was prepared to show the world what this brash young man was capable of accomplishing. But another cross was forthcoming. In 1976, Larry's marriage, though blessed with two children, failed. He still had influence, power, and pride, but what he did not have was what he needed most. That situation was about to change.

On December 12, 1984, Larry began to experience severe headaches. Staying in bed, he knew he had to be ready for an upcoming trial. The following day, which he now recalls as the feast day of Our Lady of Guadalupe, Larry was in court to present his case. Suddenly, the thirty-six-year-old attorney collapsed. He was rushed to the hospital, where he was diagnosed with a stroke. Larry had hit bottom.

While in the hospital, Larry cried out, "Please help me." At that moment, the hot-shot attorney, Notre Dame football hero suddenly realized that there was someone missing in his life. And that someone was God. It was not long before the Lord sent His ambassadors. There was the patient in the bed next to Larry who talked about the mercy of Christ. A nurse's aide gently chided the stricken patient to have faith. Others would drop in and encourage the young attorney to pray that the Holy Spirit might heal his heart. And then there was a visiting priest in the hospital who strongly encouraged Larry to return to the sacraments. For the first time in fifteen years Larry received the Eucharist. It was Christmas week, and many Christians had set the stage for Larry's return to God.

A short time later another priest, Father Norm Douglas, entered Larry's life. It was Father Norm who helped

Larry realize that the death of a father, illness of a brother, broken marriage, and troublesome profession were not ways in which God had struck him down. The problem had been Larry himself. He had to come to the realization that the God whom Larry blamed for all the misfortunes in his life was the same God who sent His only Son to be crucified so that sinners might attain the mercy and love of Christ.

Returning to the legal profession, Larry was a changed man. Now he and Father Norm Douglas were about to do God's work. Their first assignment was to reach out to other professionals whose thirst for God was too often forgotten. In the fall of 1986, Larry and his partner, Father Norm, started "Heart to Heart Communications", an organization dedicated to spiritual development in the workplace. Through a series of inspirational programs, "Heart to Heart Communications" touched the souls of hundreds of executives throughout the Midwest. Those who received the Heart to Heart message encouraged personal growth, friendship, reconciliation, concern for others, and ethical/purposeful living.

Today, Larry is a successful partner in a major law firm. He also continues to work for "Heart to Heart Communications", calling upon the Sacred Heart of Jesus and the Immaculate Heart of Mary for help in serving others.

Larry often comes across people whose personal crucifixions and resurrections mirror his own. When this happens, Larry can only smile, knowing that the God he finally forgave has forgiven him too.

PART III

The Purification

THE RESURRECTION

Kairos

I T was a simple life, really. A carpenter by trade, Joseph could support the raising of a family in his hometown of Nazareth. So, following Jewish custom, he was betrothed to a young girl named Mary. But as Joseph soon found out, all his plans were to change.

One day when Joseph was visiting Mary, a short time before the wedding was to take place, she filled him in on a little secret. She was pregnant! Not only was she carrying someone else's child, but there was something about the miraculous intervention by the Holy Spirit. Now imagine for a moment what it must have been like for Joseph, who at the time was known for two things: one, he was a good carpenter; two, he was a righteous man. He was crushed.

He was also frightened for his bride-to-be, for he knew that the punishment for adultery was death.

Unwilling to expose her "sin", Joseph planned to divorce the young girl quietly, hoping that she would not be harmed for her indiscretion. And then something happened. Joseph had a dream in which the angel of the Lord appeared to him and said: "Joseph, son of David, do not be afraid to take Mary your wife into your home. For it is through the Holy Spirit that this child has been conceived in her. She will bear a son and you are to name Him Jesus, because He will save His people from their sins." When Joseph awoke, he had a decision to make: Believe the angel in the dream, who confirmed what Mary had told him, or write off the whole experience as mystical nonsense. Joseph trusted in God. He agreed to marry the young virgin, recognizing that she might well be carrying the Messiah.

As if he did not have enough to worry about, later Joseph received the news that he would have to travel with his betrothed to Bethlehem, his birthplace, to fulfill the government's decree that all residents must be registered. It was one thing to make a dangerous journey with a band of friends, quite another to travel alone with a pregnant teenager who just might be carrying the Son of God in her womb! But Joseph had faith. He would need it.

Arriving in Bethlehem, his first responsibility was to find a place where he and Mary could stay. The situation became all the more urgent as he knew that Mary could deliver her child at any time. But Joseph's search was futile, as he experienced one rejection after another. There was no room in the inn. The only choice left was to accept an offer to sleep in a stable where the animals were kept. One cannot help but wonder how he felt. Here he was, responsible for Mary and her unborn child, and he could not even provide a decent roof over their heads. What choice did he have?

After entering the stable, Mary gave birth to Jesus. For Joseph, the miracle of the moment helped him forget the dire circumstances they were facing: the poor accommodations, loneliness, and isolation. The loneliness would not last long. Suddenly, there were shepherds outside the stable. "May we see the child?" they asked. Joseph had to make another decision. Should he let strangers approach his family? How did they know Jesus had just been born? Was the angel who told the "good news" to the visitors the same one who had appeared to him in the dream? Did it matter?

The mystery would continue some time later, when three wealthy men from far-away lands would, like their predecessors, the shepherds, ask if they could see the child. Again, Joseph would have to make a decision few men would make. He would have to trust that these events were part of a greater plan.

Forty days after Jesus' birth, Joseph and Mary took the child to the temple to be circumcised according to Jewish law. Another mystery was about to occur. A man named Simeon, upon holding the child, revealed that the "promised one" was now with his people. And if that were not enough, Simeon said to Mary, "Behold this child is destined for the fall and rise of many in Israel, and to be a sign that will be contradicted, and you yourself a sword will pierce." These were strong words for any family man to accept. But for Joseph, his faith in God would carry the day.

Another change was in the works. One night, shortly after the visit of the wise men, Joseph had another dream. This time, the angel of the Lord came to him and said: "Rise, take the child and His mother, flee to Egypt, and stay there until I tell you. Herod is going to search for the child to destroy Him." Once again, Joseph had to trust God, knowing that this would mean that his family would have to settle in a land far from Israel. Joseph's decision was providential, as the evil king murdered hundreds of infants in what is now known as the "slaughter of the innocents".

Joseph was a simple man whom God called on to protect and raise the Son of the Most High. To accomplish this mission, Joseph had to encounter a *kairos* experience. *Kairos* is a Greek term meaning "in God's time". And for the carpenter of Galilee, God's time demanded that His servant Joseph undergo a "resurrection of faith" necessary to fulfill a prophecy: "But you, O Bethlehem Ephrathah, who are little to be among the clans of Judah, from you shall come forth for me one who is to be ruler in Israel" (Mic 5:2).

"If Christ Be *Not* Risen"

If someone were to ask you what are the five most important things in your life, aside from things needed for basic survival, such as air, water, food, sun, and so on, how would you answer? If that same person asked you to put these five selections in order of importance, which one would come out on top? Since necessities are excluded, you probably would list five things that make you happy. If "happiness" is the goal, then you may want to choose from the list below:

- Money: Can you be happy without it?
- Relationships: Doesn't everyone want to have someone to love?
- Health: Without your health, what do you really have?
- Vocation: How can you get where you want to go without a path to follow?
- Talent: Won't you need certain gifts to get there?
- Family: Whom will you count on when your friends have left you?
- Faith: Without God in your life, can you really be happy?
- Physical appeal: Don't attractive people have more opportunities?
- Connections: Isn't it "who you know" that counts?
- Intelligence: GPAs, SATs, ACTs . . . enough said.
- Popularity: Do you know anyone who does not want to be liked?

Ask yourself this question. Assuming I knew my five choices, what would I be willing to give up if forced to do so? Let's suppose that your top five were faith, family, health, relationships, and vocation. One could argue that though all are important in your search for happiness, you could still survive if you lost one or more of these gifts.

For instance, let's suppose your vocation, or "calling", is to have a singing career. You could make good money. Be famous. Touch hearts. But what would happen if you damaged your vocal chords and lost your voice? Certainly, you would be very unhappy. What if the person you were in love with decided to abandon you because you no longer made him happy? Sadness would likely set in. Let's say that the doctors discovered your injury did not just end your career but might well end your life. With cancer looming on the heels of a shattered career and loss of a loved one, you could fall into deep depression. But hopefully your family would rally around you as you face the trial of your life. What if they did not? Suppose they took the position that though they were indeed sorry about your circumstances, they did not have time to tend to your emotional and physical needs. It seems that the demands of work, their own family problems, and personal interests are reasons why you will have to just "go it alone". Now you have lost four of the most important things in your life. The only gift left is faith. It all comes down to God. For without Him, you can do nothing. With Him, nothing is impossible.

Popularity, good looks, money, fame, connections, brains, love, talent, health, and family can all be taken away. Faith is the one blessing that only *you* can give away. This is the promise of the Resurrection. Were it not so, the words of Saint Paul in his first letter to the Corinthians would ring hollow: "If Christ has not been raised, your faith is futile" (1 Cor 15:17).

"I Believe"

These two words represent the foundation of your faith. The faith of the twelve apostles, after Jesus ascended into heaven, can be summarized as follows: "I believe in God, the Father almighty, creator of heaven and earth. I believe in Jesus Christ, his only Son, our Lord. He was conceived by the power of the Holy Spirit and born of the Virgin Mary. He suffered under Pontius Pilate, was crucified, died, and was buried. He descended into hell. On the third day He rose again. He ascended into heaven and is seated at the right hand of the Father. He will come again to judge the living and the dead. I believe in the Holy Spirit, the holy catholic Church, the communion of saints, the forgiveness of sins, the resurrection of the body, and the life everlasting. Amen."

When you say these words, or those of the Nicene Creed at Mass, you are taking an oath. Do not just mumble phrases because others respond on key. If you do not believe what you are saying, why say anything? You do not want to stand before the crucifix and repeat a prayer if it does not mean anything to you; such prayers mean little to God. So the next time you have an opportunity to recite the Apostles' Creed or the Nicene Creed, make sure you believe: (1) There is a God who has created everything in this world and the next. (2) His only Son Jesus, was sent into this world to save God's people. (3) Through the Holy Spirit, Jesus was conceived and born of a virgin. (4) Jesus was eventually condemned and murdered. (5) He descended into the depths of hell, bringing hope to souls, and three days later Jesus rose from the dead. (6) Before He returned to His Father, Jesus promised to glorify those who love God and neighbor. (7) As we await the second coming of Christ, the Spirit of God will prepare us through wisdom, understanding, counsel, fortitude, knowledge, piety, and fear of the Lord. (8) The Church represents the one Holy God, who reaches out to all peoples through disciples in communion with Christ. (9) The Church includes those who are pilgrims on earth; the dead who are being purified; and the saints in heaven, who pray for us. (10) Through the grace of the Holy Spirit, sins are forgiven. (11) Those who are righteous will experience the resurrection of both body and soul. (12) They will reign with Christ for all eternity.

Those who know their Creed, live their Creed, and love their Creed are guaranteed one simple promise: In God's time you will be invited to your resurrection.

Faith 1, Football 0

Gerry had it all, a beautiful wife, loving children, and four state championships in five years. Coach Gerry Faust was one of the hottest properties in Cincinnati, Ohio. His winning record would surely lead to the next level, where he would probably land an assistant coaching position for a Division III college. But Gerry had only one dream: To become the head football coach at Notre Dame. Gerry believed. In fact, he was so sure that one day the opportunity would come that he told Father Krusling at Moeller High School that he would not renew his contract unless he had an escape clause that would allow him to accept the Notre Dame job, should it ever be offered.

Father Krusling only laughed as he handed Gerry the pen. After all, he reasoned, high school coaches, regardless of their record, never jump to the head coaching position of a Division I school without first having some college experience. And the idea that his energetic friend could become Notre Dame's head football coach ranked right up there with the parting of the Red Sea.

But Gerry had friends in high places. One day he and his wife drove up to South Bend, Indiana, to see some of their ex-Moeller athletes play for the most prestigious football program in the country. After arriving on campus, Gerry had an important stop to make. Kneeling before the Blessed Mother in the famous Notre Dame Grotto, Gerry lit the usual candles for his family and his parents. He then lit a third candle promising that if he ever got the Notre Dame coaching position, he would make personal visits every day regardless of the demands of the job. Three weeks later a phone call from Father Edmund Joyce, Notre Dame executive vice president, set in motion what many in the secular world would term a miracle. On November 25, 1980, Gerry Faust, after attending a private Mass with the president of the university, was introduced as the twenty-fourth head football coach in Notre Dame history.

Gerry's prayers had been answered. What he did not know then, but knows now, is that coaching football, like any other vocation, is nothing more than God's method for engaging his servants in the hearts, minds, and souls of others. Gerry Faust was about to experience both crucifixion and resurrection.

His job was to win, period. In fact, the president of the university was adamant: "Gerry, don't you ever cheat at Notre Dame. Win more games than you lose. I'll keep the alumni off your back, and you've got a job forever."

Gerry kept his promise as he visited our Lady every day at the grotto. Others noticed, even joked when the Mother of God failed to help her coach win football games. (Gerry's devotion to the Blessed Mother was nothing new. He had prayed eight years to her, asking that God would send the right lady into his life. God had: Marlene was her name.) On another occasion, at the grotto he met a lovely young student who was terribly homesick. After finding out that she came from the same city as one of his players, Gerry offered to introduce them to each other. He would later recall, "Some people would consider this butting into the lives of the players. But I never thought of it that way: I saw someone who needed help, and I helped." (Apparently it worked, as that couple married and now have four children.) On another occasion, Gerry lit a special candle for a young high school football player from Cincinnati who was in a coma. Three weeks later Gerry received news from the boy's parents that he had come out of the coma. But the real news was that when the boy woke up his first words were: "Mom, Dad, I love you." As Gerry said, "This, I thought, is what life and families are about. Sticking together, through good and bad. Being there for one another." Gerry has remained friends with this young man and his family for sixteen years.

To some degree, Gerry Faust did not fit. It was not just the grotto visits, or going the extra mile to help strangers, it was the simple humility so uncommon among men in his position. One day, Gerry was gently chided by the athletic director for picking up the towels and being the last one left to turn out the lights. "There's something you've got to learn. You're the Notre Dame football coach, Gerry. You're not a manager. You've got to quit picking up towels and turning off lights." Gerry would later recall: "Nobody feared Gerry Faust, and that hurt me as a college coach."

Over the next five years Gerry experienced the highs and lows of college coaching. He did win more than he lost. He touched the hearts of many players, students, employees, and alumni. But in the end, Gerry Faust could not deliver a national championship for the University of Notre Dame. Art Decio, a member of the Board of Trustees, stated what many felt. "How could anyone say that Gerry Faust, with his values, didn't add to Notre Dame? He did." Mr. Decio was not alone in his praise for Gerry. Tom Osborn, Nebraska's head football coach, said that he admired Gerry for the Christian demeanor that the coach displayed during adversity. Syndicated columnist Ann Landers wrote: "You conducted yourself like a gentleman, kept the standards high, never whined, never complained, never passed the buck and always behaved in a way that brought honor to Notre Dame. In my book, you are a winner." The actor Martin Sheen echoed these sentiments: "You demonstrated far more courage and strength of character in defeat than any coach has ever shown in victory."

Perhaps the best compliments can only come from those who were put in your charge. Rusty Lisch, former Notre Dame quarterback, wrote: "Your love of our Lord, your devotion to Mary will not wane as He sends you crosses (in whatever form), but will be opportunities to come close to Him and His life of suffering." And from Wally Kleine, Notre Dame defensive tackle, "It's too bad that coaches are judged on their win-loss record, because even though that record was not what we would have liked, your record as a man is 100 percent winner. I've been very proud and happy to have been able to spend four years with you. I feel very fortunate in that not only are you my coach, you are my friend forever. I love you."

Within one week of Gerry's resignation, he received eight offers from colleges around the country who were all interested in the man who could not win a national championship for Notre Dame. He eventually ended up in Akron, Ohio, where he took on the daunting task of elevating their virtually unknown program.

Though Gerry moved away from the university that honored the Mother of God, he never moved away from her. Visiting Lourdes and Fatima (famous Marian apparition sites), Gerry continued to strengthen his bond with Mary. The realities of what is really important in life hit home at each stop in his journey. In Fatima, he saw crippled bodies but strong faith. At Lourdes, he met a man who was dying of cancer. When Gerry mentioned that perhaps this fellow might experience a miraculous healing, the man smiled and pointed to a group of children in wheelchairs. "If a miracle is going to happen, let it happen to one of them. They haven't lived their lives."

The legacy of Coach Gerry Faust was written long before he took Moeller High School to so many state championships, long before he made a quantum leap, coaching the most recognized college football program in the country, and long before he visited the most famous Marian shrines in the world. Gerry's legacy began to be scripted in his prayer life, daily Mass, and recitations of the rosary. His undying devotion to the Blessed Mother led him to Marlene, Notre Dame, and the hundreds of souls he would touch along his journey of faith. From sorrow to joy, crucifixion to resurrection, Gerry Faust will be the first one to tell you that God was with him every step of the way.

A few days after Gerry Faust's football career ended in Akron, Ohio, he attended morning Mass. At the conclusion of the Mass the pastor, Father Yahner, spontaneously addressed his congregation: "Thanks for Gerry Faust. He may be taken away from the football field but he'll never be taken away from the table of the Lord." At that moment, this author, along with everyone else, stood and applauded the man of whom Regis Philbin wrote: "Gerry Faust will tell you he may not have been the right coach for Notre Dame but he was the right man. He still is."

THE ASCENSION

The Diary

HELENA Kowalska was born in Lodz, Poland, on August 25, 1905, the third of ten children. In her childhood, she was noticed for her fervent prayer, obedience to her parents, and sensitivity toward the poor. Her love of God led her to the Congregation of the Sisters of Our Lady of Mercy. At the age of twenty-one, she received her habit and accepted the name Sister Maria Faustina of the Most Blessed Sacrament. For the next five years, Sister Faustina performed menial tasks while asking Jesus for the opportunity to offer her life for the salvation of lost souls.

On February 22, 1931, Sister Faustina had a mystical vision of Jesus. The Lord told her: "Paint an image according to the pattern you see with the signature: Jesus, I Trust in You." He went on to say, "I desire that this image be venerated, first in your chapel, and then throughout the world. I promise that the soul who will venerate this image will not perish. I also promise victory over enemies already here on earth, especially at the hour of death. I Myself will defend it as My own glory."

Startled, Sister Faustina immediately shared her experience with her confessor, who told her to, "Paint God's image in your soul." But upon leaving the confessional she heard another voice: "My image is already in your soul. I desire that there be a Feast of Mercy." Jesus further stated, "I want this image which you will paint with a brush to be solemnly blessed on the first Sunday after Easter; that Sunday is to be the Feast of Mercy."

Sister Faustina had two problems. First, you do not just pick up the phone and call the Pope, instructing him that the Son of God has put in an order. Second, the good Sister could not paint! Speaking with her Mother Superior, she received the expected, "Let's see if Jesus gives you some sign that will allow us to recognize Him more clearly." Now it is easy to accuse the religious authorities for not trusting in the words of Christ. But one must be careful when presented with an unbelievable story.

Troubled, Sister Faustina begged her confessor to give her the words that would remove such responsibilities from her soul. He would not. Rather, he advised Sister Faustina to get a personal spiritual advisor. This direction would eventually lead her to Father Sopocko, who told Sister Faustina to start recording all interior conversations and visions in a diary. He also helped her find the painter needed to depict the Divine Mercy on canvas. And it was

Father Sopocko who said of Sister Faustina as she was near death, "She looked like an unearthly being. At that time I no longer had the slightest doubt that what she had written in her diary about receiving Holy Communion from an angel was really true."

Over the next seven years, Sister Faustina would record her conversations with Jesus, Mary, and her guardian angel. She would also describe the suffering she endured for other souls, which was witnessed by both her superior and confessor. And most importantly, Sister Faustina would provide future readers with a road map leading to the Chaplet of the Divine Mercy.

Sister Faustina's ascension to the Divine Mercy would lead to hundreds of mystical encounters. On more than one occasion, a soul from Purgatory visited the nun asking for her prayers. After the good sister prayed to the Divine Mercy, that same soul would communicate with Sister Faustina, thanking her for her intervention.

Jesus told Sister Faustina that before He returns as the last judge, He will first return as the King of Mercy. To that end, Jesus predicted: "The sign of the cross will be seen in the sky, and from the openings where the hands and the feet of the Savior were nailed, will come forth great lights which will light up the earth for a period of time. This will take place shortly before the last day."

The Visions

Sister Faustina recorded many visions, most of which few would care to see. She witnessed Christ on the Cross, His crown of thorns, His blood and tears. She encountered evil creatures that cursed at her for her devotion to the

Son of God. She saw an angel who was ready to strike the earth for the people's offenses against God, but was held back through the mercy of the Lord. She even dared to ask Jesus how He could tolerate so many sins and crimes and not punish those responsible. He responded: "I have eternity for punishing, and so I am prolonging the time of mercy for the sake of sinners." But Jesus also warned: "But woe to them if they do not recognize this time of My visitation."

Sister Faustina also experienced hell. There was hell on earth, as some of the sisters were jealous and accused her of being a "hysterical visionary". One nun said bluntly: "Get it out of your head, Sister, that the Lord Jesus might be communing in such an intimate way with such a miserable bundle of imperfections as you!"

But the other hell, the real hell, was worst of all. In one horrible vision, Sister Faustina was led by an angel to the very depths of the underworld, where souls of sinners were in great anguish, knowing they would never see God. A place of continual darkness, it was filled with a suffocating smell, tears of despair, torment of the senses, and other tortures so terrible that Sister Faustina could barely write the words, "I would have died at the very sight of these tortures if the omnipotence of God had not supported me."

Two other points are worth noting. Sister Faustina recorded that most of the souls who were lost were the same ones who on earth had laughed at the idea of a hell. She also recorded that many souls in hell were the same ones who on earth had received awards and applause.

In Luke 16:19-31, Jesus tells the story of a rich man who asked God to warn his brothers about the reality of hell, of which he was now a resident. In the parable, Abraham responds to the man with this warning: "They have Moses and the prophets; let them hear them." But the rich man cries out one final time: "No, father Abraham; but if some one goes to them from the dead, they will repent." At this, Abraham says: "If they do not hear Moses and the prophets, neither will they be convinced if some one should rise from the dead." The "some one" Abraham was referring to was Jesus, whose Resurrection would be denied soon after and, too often, is denied now.

Of all her visions, there was none more important than one of Jesus, where rays of light streamed from His Sacred Heart. With the help of Father Sopocko, an artist was commissioned to paint the image as described by Sister Faustina. When the nun finally saw the finished product, she wept, acknowledging that no human hands could capture the beauty of the merciful Christ. During her tears she suddenly heard the words, "Not in the beauty of the color nor of the brush lies the greatness of this image, but in My grace."

When asked later the meaning of the colored rays in the picture, Sister Faustina relayed what Jesus said: "The two rays denote blood and water. The pale ray stands for the Water, which makes souls righteous. The red ray stands for the Blood which is the life of souls." Jesus went on to say, "These two rays issued forth from the very depths of My tender mercy when My agonized Heart was opened by a lance on the Cross." Today, almost seventy years later, the Divine Mercy image with the words "Jesus, I Trust in You" is frequently displayed when the Chaplet of the Divine Mercy, the special prayer our Lord gave Sister Faustina, is recited.

Sister Faustina died on October 5, 1938, at the age of thirty-three. On April 18, 1993, Pope John Paul II beatified the Polish nun. Seven years later, she became the first saint of the new millennium when the Holy Father canonized Sister Faustina on Sunday, April 30, 2000. The choice of this Sunday was in response to a diary entry dated November 5, 1934. On that day, our Lord specifically requested that the feast of the Divine Mercy be celebrated every year on the first Sunday following Easter. For those who celebrate the Divine Mercy, their ascension cannot be far behind.

"O God, Be Merciful to Me a Sinner"

This request comes directly from Luke 18:13, in Jesus' parable about the Pharisee and tax collector who were in the temple to pray. The Pharisee took his rightful place in front and then stated: "God, I thank you that I am not like other men, extortioners, unjust, adulterers, or even like this tax collector." But the tax collector stood off at a distance and would not even raise his eyes to heaven but beat his breast and prayed for the mercy of God. At the end of the parable, Jesus gave this warning: "Every one who exalts himself will be humbled, but he who humbles himself will be exalted."

To ensure that you fall in the latter category, it would be

best to conduct an examination of your conscience. One way to conduct an honest review of what you have done, or failed to do, is to compare your performance with the rules of heaven, better known as the Ten Commandments.

Rule 1. There is one God and you shall have no other gods before Him.

Do you give Him the time He requests of you? Do you pray? Do you offer your day to Him? Have you read His story? Do you know His saints? Are you familiar with the teachings of His Church? Are you caught up in the worship of other gods, which include money, fame, sex, or possessions? Have you explored the world of the occult?

Rule 2. You shall not take the name of the Lord your God in vain.

Do you swear in anger using the name of God? Have you broken a vow you made to God? Have you ever spoken ill of God, blaming Him for your circumstances?

Rule 3. Remember the Sabbath Day to keep it holy.

Do you attend Mass every Sunday? Do you pay attention to the readings, the sermon, and the ceremony? Do you give this day to the Lord?

Rule 4. Honor your father and your mother.

Do you obey your parents? Are you grateful for all they have tried to do for you and the rest of the family? Have you offered to help them out whether they ask or not? Have you done your part to keep the family together?

Rule 5. You shall not kill.

Easy, you say. Have you ever physically injured someone? Have you failed to stand up for the "sanctity of life", choosing instead to argue for the right to abortion or euthanasia? Have you ever participated in alcohol or drug abuse, both of which have the power to kill the body and the soul? Have you harbored hatred, anger, or vengeance toward another, wishing them ill? Have you failed to be a "peacemaker" of God?

Rule 6. You shall not commit adultery.

Have you engaged in any inappropriate sexual activity? Have you satisfied your lust with pornographic movies, books, magazines, or videos? Do you enjoy telling obscene jokes? Do you endorse homosexual behavior? Have you violated another person or tempted an individual to participate in immoral behavior?

Rule 7. You shall not steal.

Have you ever cheated on a test? Do you steal from friends, family, or strangers? Do you do the job that is expected of you at work, in school, or on the athletic field? Have you respected what belongs to others? Have you been faithful in your obligations? Do you give to the poor?

Rule 8. You shall not bear false witness against your neighbor.

Do you lie? Have you gossiped about or slandered another? Have you tried to ruin the reputation of someone you did not like? Do you tolerate condemnation of another person's race, color, or religion? Have you withheld the truth for fear of reprisal? Do you ever "rush to judgment" without giving the person a chance? Have you ever tried to rationalize immoral behavior?

Rule 9. You shall not covet your neighbor's wife.

Have you ever been disloyal to your family, choosing instead the desires of your friends? Have you encouraged the infidelity of one of your parents? Have you taken sides in family disputes so that you could get your way? Have you supported moral permissiveness in your home by what you watch on television, your language, or how you dress?

Rule 10. You shall not covet your neighbor's goods.

Do you compare yourself with your friends or neighbors in terms of what you own, how you dress, or where you live? Are you jealous because this boy is popular or that girl is attractive? Do you share with those less fortunate than you? Do you remember to put some money in Sunday's collection? Are you continually distracted trying to find ways to make more money or gain more influence? Do you ever wish that this or that person would lose his job, position, or money?

Jesus once said, "For where your treasure is, there will your heart be also" (Mt 6:21). And the treasure you must seek begins with the Divine Mercy. Only He, through the Holy Spirit, can give you the grace needed to overcome the temptation of sin.

"Blessed Are the Merciful, For They Shall Obtain Mercy"

This call to action is one of the nine Beatitudes taught by Christ. One way to respond to the blessing is to honor our Lord's request to pray for souls who need special graces. In a nine-day novena of the Chaplet of the Divine Mercy, Jesus asked Sister Faustina to pray for many souls. On the first day, one should pray for all mankind. The second day is for priests and other religious who are accountable for representing the faith. The third day is dedicated to devout and faithful souls. Day four reaches out to those who do not know Christ or the mercy He offers. On the fifth day, novena participants are asked to remember those souls who try to disrupt the teachings of Christ and His Church. On the sixth day, the meek and humble, particularly children, are invited to His mercy. The seventh day is reserved for those who venerate the Divine Mercy. The eighth day belongs to souls in Purgatory as they anxiously await their departure for heaven. Finally, on the ninth day, our Lord reaches out to the greatest number of souls who are "lukewarm" in their faith and love of God.

If you seek His mercy, receive the sacraments, and remember others in your prayers, you will be well on your way to your ascension in Christ.

The Cross

Joseph Krupp was the youngest of six children. He was also a favorite of the "adopted" brothers who at one time or another stayed with the family. One of the guests was a Muslim named Abdul, who helped teach young Joseph to pray. One time when Abdul was about to leave for the summer, he found Joseph crying over the loss of his

Muslim friend. Abdul picked Joseph up and said: "Joe, I'm only going away for a little while. You know I'm coming back." Joseph looked up and through his tears retorted: "My heart doesn't know what my head does." Their friendship remains some twenty-five years later.

Mom and Dad Krupp were the architects of a loving home that made prayer the center of their lives. Joseph remembers the family gathering every night to say their evening prayers. He remembers how each person was asked to read from Holy Scripture and then pass the "good book" to the next in line. Even at the age of five, he was invited to spread the Word of God. He could not read, but his family did not mind. God did not mind either when Joseph would open the big book and begin preaching thirty-second sermons.

The Krupp parents were two of fifty other parents who made a serious commitment to prayer. At their church, the children of these families represented the majority of altar servers and choir members. Dads were ushers. Moms ran the religious education classes. These families set an example for what the "church community" embodies.

As Joseph grew up, he became aware that other people in town thought that their little prayer group was a cult. Joseph, like many of his friends, found himself in school fights merely because he was "different". It was not uncommon to hear teachers make remarks about the cult families and their "brainwashed" kids. Joseph found it ironic that the school administration would tolerate young people painting their bodies in school colors, but could not tolerate him and his friends taking their faith seriously.

When the church community lost their priest, a new pastor was assigned. The battle to practice one's faith was now spreading beyond the classroom walls and into the very house of God. The new priest announced that the community had to submit to his leadership, condemning any parishioner charismatic behavior. Joseph's family and all other families who participated in group prayer sessions were forbidden to serve in any church capacity. Joseph and his family were living the ninth Beatitude. "Blessed are you when men revile you and persecute you and utter all kinds of evil against you falsely on my account. Rejoice and be glad, for your reward is great in heaven" (Mt 5:11–12).

The persecution included drive-by taunting, beer cans thrown in the front yard, and signs ridiculing Martha, Joseph's mom. She was even accused of being a witch. In time, Joseph and his family were forced to leave the parish they had helped build. With all Joseph experienced, he still knew one thing. He loved God, and God loved him.

The Call

On April 10, 1977, Joseph was asked to take his turn and read from the Bible. The little seven-year-old opened the book and found his tiny finger pointing to John 6:10. The passage read: "There is a lad here who has five barley loaves and two fish; but what are they among so many?" As one little boy read about another little boy, the seeds of Holy Orders were sown. Even Joseph's mom mentioned that her little son was being called to the priesthood.

Later, as a teenager facing condemnation for living a life of prayer, Joseph found it hard to pursue his vocation actively without harboring ill will toward the very institution that was calling him, but Joseph's position on the matter was clear. "I loved Jesus and was going to be a priest."

At a national gathering of Charismatics in Indianapolis, Indiana, the "call" to the priesthood was extended. A bishop there challenged all young men present who contemplated becoming a priest to approach the altar. Joseph sat there quietly until suddenly another young man, to whom Joseph looked up, tapped him on the shoulder and said, "C'mon, let's go." Joseph walked forward and never looked back. The bishop came up to Joseph and said: "Joe, you've been ducking this for a long time. Make up your mind. You can tell God yes, or you can tell God no. He can work with either, but not both." At that moment, God placed the call, and Joseph answered.

The Mother

"Jesus is enough for me." Those words represented Joseph's response to the question of why Mary, the Blessed Mother, did not play a role in the young seminarian's life. To Joseph, God was always accessible, so why waste time going through the "middleman (woman)"? An experience in Denver would forever change Joseph's understanding of, and love for, the Mother of God.

At a place called Cherry Creek Park, Joseph and several other young people were taking a hike. It was extremely cold, and he was doing his best to control his shivering. As the group walked along the path, one of the leaders came up to Joseph and started talking to him about the Holy Mother. After a short conversation the gentleman asked, "Don't you think it's about time you prayed to Mary?" Joseph was still resistant. At that moment, one of the teenage girls came up to Joseph and asked: "Would you pray for me? I really think Mary is trying to tell me something." Though her request startled him, he joined hands with the rest of those present and prayed. "Mary, I've never talked to you before. I'm sorry. Please do something."

His prayer was all he could offer. But what the Blessed Mother was about to offer would change Joseph's heart forever. During the group prayer, the other leader spoke up. "Mary, wrap your mantle around him." Joseph was suddenly warm. Someone had just covered him up with the burning fire of love. And like a child whose tears are kissed by a mother's love, so too were Joseph's tears. It did not matter that the young seminarian was crying. Everyone understood.

A second Marian incident involved Joseph's grandmother. Joseph recalls that Grandma would frequently pray her rosary. One day, when he was working at a hospital, he went up to the nursing home floor where he stopped in to see a patient. She was affectionately known as Miss Elizabeth. This kindly woman never let her rosary out of her hands. And though Joseph had never mentioned his grandma, he could not help noticing that the elderly woman had a rosary very similar to the one his grandmother used. One day he mentioned the coincidence to Miss Elizabeth, and the woman suddenly said: "Oh, son, your grandma's sick, and she's going to see God today. Get home."

Joseph's fear was confirmed when the chaplain's office

called to tell him that his mother needed him to get home at once. Joseph's grandmother was dying. The traffic was terrible. The weather was bad. Joseph knew he was too late. His grandmother had passed away ten minutes before he arrived. As he knelt over her to kiss her goodbye, members of the family recalled the moments before she passed away. Though Grandma was in a coma, the sound of her granddaughter playing the hymn "Ave Maria" suddenly caused the dying woman to sit up and join her family in the Hail Mary. When they arrived at the words "now and at the hour of our death", Grandma closed her eyes and died.

Joseph's love for Jesus took a step back because of his disappointment. He rationalized that since God could not wait ten minutes, Joseph did not have time for God. A short time later, Joseph was challenged by a fellow seminarian to consider that Mary was Jesus' representative advocating for the mercy of God. Joseph now understood. Mary was sent by her Son.

Father Joe's spiritual journey began with his love of Jesus. Along the way, he learned to love his Savior's Mother. Together, Jesus and Mary continue to lead their priest to his ascension.

PENTECOST

Touched by a Soldier

DURING the Korean War, there was an incident that was reported by a soldier named Corporal Michael Frank. One day as his squad was about to venture into enemy territory, he noticed that there was a new recruit he had never seen before. Corporal Frank learned that the stranger had just joined the platoon and that he too was named Michael. Moving forward, the squad suddenly came under intense fire from an overwhelming force. The corporal was wounded and was rapidly losing consciousness. Preparing to die, the young soldier was whispering a prayer when suddenly the battlefield around him was filled with intense light. Nearly blinded, he witnessed what looked like an ancient warrior swinging a shining sword at enemy troops as they moved in for the kill. A short time later he found himself surrounded by the rest of the platoon, demanding to know how he was able to kill so many enemy soldiers. "It wasn't me", he stammered. "It was the new guy, the tall one named Michael, the one with the sword." "Get him back to the base, he's delirious", the platoon leader barked out. "But what about Michael, is he all right?" There was no reply.

Was the stranger Michael the Archangel? For the soldier who reported the story, there was no doubt who had saved his life. At her trial, Joan of Arc was prepared to be executed rather than deny her "voices", one of which was that of this Archangel. Over the years there have been many accounts of the assistance of angels and their leader, Michael, whose name means "Who is like God?". Michael the Archangel and his companions are servants of God, and they help us by protecting us from evil.

In Revelation 12:7–9, the Apostle John records his vision of good and evil. "Now war arose in heaven, Michael and his angels fighting against the dragon; and the dragon and his angels fought, but they were defeated and there was no longer any place for them in heaven. And the great dragon was thrown down, the ancient serpent, who is called the Devil and Satan, the deceiver of the whole world—he was thrown down to earth, and his angels were thrown down with him."

Throughout history, there have been many accounts of angels coming to the aid of those whose battle with evil requires the assistance of a higher power. Perhaps the best modern drama illustrating this point is the movie *It's a Wonderful Life*. In this film a man named George Bailey has a bad run of luck. When he is in total despair, his enemy suggests that the only way out of his mess is to commit suicide. George seriously contemplates taking his life, telling himself that it would have been better if he had never been born. At that moment, his guardian angel intervenes by granting the man's wish. "So you think life would have been better without you?" the angel asks. "Very well, you've got your wish!"

George discovers that the pharmacist whom he had stopped from mixing the wrong prescription ended up poisoning a youth. When his little brother fell through the ice, he drowned because George was not there to save him. The town flirt ended up a prostitute because George was not there to help her in her darkest hour. The greedy entrepreneur destroyed many families because George was not there to help them in their time of need. And the beautiful family he had in life never existed because George Bailey never existed.

At the sight of these tragedies, George cries out, "I want to live again." And with the help of his guardian angel, he is given a second chance. At the end of the story that second chance results in a tremendous outpouring of love from all the people George Bailey helped during his life, a life that was saved by an angel.

Imagine how George felt when he knew he was alive again with the entire town coming to his home to give back to him the same love he gave to them. The euphoria in his heart had to be overwhelming.

Now imagine how the apostles felt when suddenly, "a sound came from heaven like the rush of a mighty wind, and it filled all the house where they were sitting. And there appeared to them tongues as of fire, distributed and resting on each one of them. And they were all filled with the Holy Spirit" (Acts 2:2).

For the soldier in Korea, for the fictional George Bailey, and for the apostles, the time of Pentecost had arrived. And sooner or later, your Pentecost will arrive. At that hour you can bet that your guardian angel will be present. In the meantime, you may want to memorize a prayer that reaches out to the one angel whom God has appointed the leader of the forces of heaven, in their triumph over the powers of hell.

"Holy Michael, the Archangel, defend us in the day of battle; be our safeguard against the wickedness and snares of the devil. May God rebuke him, we humbly pray; and do thou, Prince of the heavenly Host, by the power of God thrust down to hell Satan and all wicked spirits, who wander through the world seeking the ruin of souls." Amen.

"Though I Walk in the Valley of Death"

Evil exists. Satan exists. Hell exists. All three are interrelated. Unfortunately, many young people choose to deny the possibility that evil spirits will do anything to get you to doubt their existence. If you do not believe in eternal damnation, then you might as well do as you please. If there are no consequences to your behavior, why behave?

If the Ten Commandments are only suggestions, why not pick and choose which one you will follow? That way you do not have to worry about breaking any rules. If the Bible is only a fictional story, why bother to study this so-called Word of God? If Jesus did not die for our sins, then what was the point of His death?

A philosopher once argued for believing in the existence of God by using some rather interesting logic. He stated that if God exists and you choose to believe in Him, you are going to be fine. If God does not exist and you still believe in Him, you are not going to get in trouble. But if you choose not to believe in God and there is a God, you are in real danger.

Enter the Holy Spirit. Through the grace of the Third Person of the Trinity, you will receive both divine love and protection. When the apostles experienced their Pentecost, they suddenly had the courage needed to face their adversaries. They had the inspiration to preach, regardless of the consequences. And they had the conviction that the teachings of Jesus Christ were the eternal blueprint for truth.

"But for the grace of God there go I" is a popular reminder that God, His angels, and His saints are there to help you fight "the ten commandments of evil". These are lies fed to young people over most of today's world.

1. Thou shalt *always* be tolerant of others' values, behavior, or morality.
   Counterpoint: To be tolerant means to be accepting of what is *good*, even if you have no particular interest in the topic, activity, person, or outcome. Never defend another person's "right" to be immoral.

2. Thou shalt always accept anyone's definition of what a "family" is.

   Counterpoint: For more than two thousand years a family has been defined as a mother, father, and their offspring, either biological or adopted. Family extensions included grandparents, aunts, uncles, and cousins. Any attempts to redefine the very tapestry of our society will only result in a greater tolerance of evil.

3. Thou shalt remember that the problems of today's generation are no different from the problems other generations faced.

   Counterpoint: There have always been teen pregnancy, alcohol and drug abuse, crime, and other societal ills. What has changed is the false tolerance (that word again) society has for these problems. Parents hire lawyers when their son or daughter does not make the team. Coaches recruit convicted felons. Teachers pass students who did not do the work. Politicians condemn the entertainment industry for producing trashy programming, then turn around and accept political contributions from the same group. Supreme Court justices begin each session with the words, "God save us and the honorable court", then prohibit prayer at football games.

4. Thou shalt never forget that "freedom is just another word for nothing else to lose."

   Counterpoint: Freedom without responsibility is a prescription for personal, psychological, and spiritual disaster.

5. Thou shalt get what you want, when you want it.

   Counterpoint: Hedonism, or the seeking of pleasure, is self-serving and a ticket to immorality. Advertising slogans like "have it your way" and "who says you can't have it all" represent typical enticements many young people fall victim to. When someone says you can be anything you want to be, correct them by stating: "No, I can be the best I can be." If you achieve that goal, God will take care of the rest.

6. Remember, you are going to do it anyway.

    Counterpoint: Do not let anyone tell you alcohol, drugs, and sexual desire cannot be controlled. With the grace of God you can overcome any temptation. And do not let anyone convince you that because you were brought up in a particular environment, you are destined to repeat the cycle over again. There are countless examples of young people who grew up in a troubled home but managed to raise a happy, spiritually healthy family. The reverse is also true. There are untold numbers of "privileged" youth who, although growing up in what appeared to be a good home, took a wrong turn in life. Though they had access to all the world offered, they never had time for God.

7. It's not your fault.

    Counterpoint: When it is your fault, say so. When you fail, do not blame others. Do not fall into the same trap that many adults do, blaming everyone else for their failings.

8. Thou shalt search for enlightenment through a higher consciousness.

    Counterpoint: Garbage! Search for God through His Holy Spirit and through the sacraments of His Church and you will find truth. Search for evil, and it will find you!

9. Thou shalt *always* defend both freedom of speech and freedom of choice.

   Counterpoint: See number four on this list. Remember, freedom of speech has been carried to an extreme, allowing anyone to espouse hatred, lies, and vulgarity. And its cousin, freedom of choice, has led to the slaughter of forty million babies in the womb. It is one thing to speak truth; it is quite another to conceal it.

10. At all costs, maintain separation of church and state.

    Counterpoint: Teens who choose God choose morality. Those who have chosen to separate from God have chosen chaos. Do not abdicate your rights. Demand a moral society. Courts, schools, politicians, media, and many parents have made their choice. It is time for young people to make theirs. On one hand, political leadership will tell teenagers that America is the greatest country on earth. Then many of these same adults will try to do everything possible to avoid thanking the Creator who blessed this land. Remind them of these words: "Praise be to God" (Washington Monument), "Nation under God" (Lincoln Memorial), "Liberty is a gift of God" (Jefferson Memorial), "Endowed by our Creator" (Declaration of Independence), "One nation under God" (Pledge of Allegiance), "God shed His grace on thee" ("America the Beautiful"). Finally, take out your coins and read the inscription. "In God We Trust" has been this country's motto since it won its independence. Do not be independent from the One who gave you this great country.

Pray to the Holy Spirit for wisdom, and you will receive the grace necessary to do the will of God. When temptations come, ask your guardian angel and Saint Michael to defend you. Say the rosary, and Mary, the Mother of God, will be there to protect you. Ask Jesus for mercy, and mercy will be yours. Follow these simple steps, and you will be surprised to see who stops by on the day you celebrate your Pentecost.

In Search of Somebody

The seven-year-old boy was wandering in his grand-mother's garden when he noticed a young beautiful woman staring at him. She smiled and simply said: "Johnny!" Embarrassed, he looked away and ran into the house. Years later, he would remember the pleasing aroma of lilacs that filled the garden that day.

John Corapi wanted to be "somebody". An exceptional high school athlete and good student, he knew he would be successful. After graduation John decided to make his mark and joined the elite Green Berets. With his military training and a black belt in karate, John was ready to be "somebody". But an injury kept him out of the Vietnam conflict.

After his military discharge he became a certified public accountant and headed to Las Vegas, where he audited casinos. But John knew the real money to be made was in California real estate. It was not long before John Corapi was a multimillionaire. In his mind he was "somebody". He could prove it. All you had to do was visit his home on the ocean, ride in his red Ferrari, or sail in his sixty-foot yacht. Perhaps one would catch a glimpse of him as he drove with pride down Rodeo Drive.

Then one evening at a Hollywood party, he was chatting with an up-and-coming actress who offered to introduce John to her "best friend". Its name was cocaine! The fast life had begun. It was not long before John's habit was costing him ten thousand dollars a week. And shortly thereafter, the man who wanted to be "somebody" became nobody. His so-called friends disappeared. He lost his company, the Ferrari, oceanfront property, and yacht. He almost lost his life.

For one year he was a patient in a VA hospital. At his lowest point he was so sick that he wanted to die. Lying in his bed in total despair he thought he smelled the aroma of lilacs. At that moment, a beautiful nurse walked into his room, looked at the patient, and simply said, "Johnny". She smiled and then left.

A short time later, John Corapi was discharged from the hospital. But with no money and little hope, there was nothing else he could do except walk the streets of Los Angeles. His new friends were the homeless. Sometimes he would sit on a park bench facing the executive office building where he had once run his business. John Corapi was experiencing his "dark night of the soul".

Three thousand miles away there was someone who was lighting a candle for the broken man. John's mother had been praying twenty years to the Blessed Mother, asking her to bring her son home.

After wandering listlessly for months, John finally accepted his mother's invitation to come back home. When he returned home he could not help thinking that he had now come full circle. He had grown up poor, and to poverty he had returned. Gently, his mother suggested that her son say one Hail Mary a day, asking the Blessed Virgin Mary to help him. He made the commitment, but only after he looked up the words. John had forgotten how to say the prayer he had learned in Catholic school. One night he surrendered. Calling out to God, he asked that the Lord take over his life. John remembers the night well. After three hours of peace, he knew that God's name was Mercy.

The next day, John announced to his mother that he wanted to go to confession. As he approached an old priest, John could not help notice that he was saying a rosary. After John had confessed his sins, the priest looked up and said: "It's amazing! The time is 3:00 P.M. This is the exact hour when our Lord died on the Cross for your sins." From that moment on, John Corapi knew he wanted to be a priest. But he had a lot of catching up to do. He attended daily Mass, said the rosary, received the sacraments, studied Holy Scripture, and prayed up to twelve hours a day.

It was not long before the man who was nobody entered the seminary. After eleven years of studying and living life as a religious, he had obtained four university degrees and graduated *summa cum laude* with a doctorate in sacred theology. John Corapi was about to become a priest. But he received a special gift: the man who had once "danced with the devil" was among a few candidates chosen to be ordained by Pope John Paul II. At his ordination, three mothers were present. His mom beamed proudly as her son received Holy Orders. A few feet away stood another "mother". Mother Teresa of Calcutta was present when John Corapi became Father John Corapi. As the procession of newly ordained priests entered Saint Peter's Square, where one hundred thousand faithful cheered for their new priests, Father John could not help noticing the beautiful young woman smiling at him. At that moment, the unmistakable smell of lilacs confirmed his suspicion that the lady who had spoken his name had now seen the fulfillment of her promise to Father Corapi's mother.

A few days later, Father John asked if it would be possible to say his first Mass in the Clementine chapel in Saint Peter's, where the relics of the first Pope lay. Though told that more than a few cardinals would like the same privilege, Father John knew our Blessed Mother could make anything happen. When an Italian cardinal could not keep his appointment to say Mass at that holy chapel, Father John knew his request would be answered. The first confession Father John ever heard was from a man who had not received the sacrament in over thirty years! A greater blessing would follow, as his own father would request that his son hear the confession of a man who had not been in the confessional for fifty years!

Father John Corapi has been recognized by his superiors as having a gift of apostolic preaching, which allows him to teach the truths of the faith with such clarity that even the hardest hearts can be brought closer to God. The former real estate tycoon whose only god was pleasure is now "somebody" who teaches Christians about the Cross of Christ, His Divine Mercy, and the *Catechism of the Catholic Church*!

Father John Corapi, through the intercession of the Blessed Virgin Mary, is now giving other souls the opportunity to renew their faith while having the courage and conviction to follow the Cross of Christ. This man has experienced his Pentecost. He invites you to do the same.

THE ASSUMPTION

The Little Way

THESE three little words describe the way to holiness exemplified by Saint Thérèse of Lisieux, sometimes known as the "Little Flower". Born in Alençon, France, on January 2, 1873, she was the youngest of five daughters. (Four other children had died at an early age.) Her mother and father were both saintly people, and they raised their daughters accordingly. Eventually four daughters would enter a Carmelite monastery with the other daughter entering a Visitation convent in Caen.

Thérèse was "daddy's little girl", and it showed. After her mother died, the youngest of the family was so spoiled that if she did any housework at all, she felt she was doing the other family members a favor. The "princess" was very sensitive, and the thought of anyone not liking her often led to tantrums. A local priest noted that when Thérèse came to confession a "flood of tears" would flow over the littlest sins.

But spoiled or not, Thérèse had her share of tragedies. Her mother died when she was four and a half. Her dad would die when Thérèse was twenty-one. When her sister Pauline left to join the convent, Thérèse became so ill that many thought she was going to die. Thérèse recalled that as the family stood around her bed praying, she saw the statue of the Blessed Virgin Mary smiling at her. At that moment, the little girl was cured.

Two other sisters left to become nuns, leaving Thérèse, her sister Céline, and her father at home. But it would not be long before Thérèse would request, even demand, that she be allowed to join the Carmelites. She had two problems: First, how could she control her emotions in an environment that calls for hard work and strict obedience? Second, she was not yet sixteen, the minimum age required to join the order. The first issue was solved when she overheard her father make a comment about his daughter's sensitivity. Instead of crying again, she finally swallowed her tears and pretended she never heard the remark. Thérèse would later write that the hour of her "conversion" occurred at that very moment, and only the power of Jesus could have given her the grace to accept the gift of humility. That "gift" was delivered on Christmas Day 1886.

The second barrier was a test to see what little Thérèse was made of. When the authorities of the Carmelite order declined to let her enter, the teenager took up the matter with the bishop. When that did not work, she went on a trip to Rome with her father and sister. She hoped to have an audience with the Pope. Told she could say nothing to the Bishop of Rome, Thérèse ignored the protocol and immediately went up to him and asked the Pontiff to step in on the matter. The Holy Father gently said, "If it is God's will, you will enter." The tiny Thérèse had to be removed by the Swiss guards. The frustrated girl, in a letter to her sister Pauline, summed up her disappointment: "Pauline, I am the Child Jesus' little ball; if he wants to smash His toy He is quite free to do so." But God did not do so, and Thérèse entered the convent at the age of fifteen.

Thérèse was about to experience the trials of a cloistered nun. Her father suffered a series of strokes, but his little "princess" was not allowed to visit her dying father. The mental anguish was so intense that Thérèse would often fall asleep praying for the grace to accept this difficult cross.

But Thérèse was determined to love God her way. On one occasion, she discovered that there was a convicted murderer who was about to be executed. Praying intensely for his soul, she soon learned that before the sentence was carried out, the criminal who had rejected previous spiritual help suddenly kissed the crucifix three times. This may have been an indication that, like the thief on the cross who asked Jesus to "remember me when you come into your kingdom", the sinner found salvation. A miracle of mercy may have come about because a teenage girl took the time to pray for a man she never knew.

In the ensuing years, the "Little Flower" did everything she could to love God in little ways. She would accept the most menial tasks. She took the blame for something she had not done. She was pleasant to those nuns who were not. She prayed for souls others would forget. She ate everything without complaining. And when asked by Sister Pauline to remain a novice to avoid political squabbles in the convent, she humbly agreed to do so. Thérèse once said, "I wanted to accomplish little things because I couldn't accomplish big things." This philosophy was her way of giving what she could to God.

In 1896, new sacrifices would be demanded. Thérèse started to cough up blood in what was the first evidence of a serious case of tuberculosis. As the days lingered her pain became so severe that only her faith saved her from the temptation to commit suicide. Even during this difficult time there were those who accused Thérèse of faking her illness. Still, she prayed for her accusers. She often talked about the work she hoped God would let her do after her death.

On September 30, 1897, the "Little Flower" died. She was twenty-four years old. Her last words summed up the story of her life: "My God, I love you."

After her death, one sister commented that there was nothing special to say about Thérèse. But future generations would disagree, as more than one million visitors a year came to her shrine in Lisieux. Sister Pauline put together her youngest sister's writings on the "little way" by which one could grow in holiness. After she mailed two thousand copies to other convents, the demand for Thérèse's teachings was so great that within six years of her death the canonization process was underway. This book, *The Story of a Soul*, remains popular today.

On May 17, 1925, just twenty-eight years after her death, Thérèse was canonized by Pope Pius XI. In 1997,

Pope John Paul II declared Saint Thérèse of Lisieux a Doctor of the Church, an honor given to fewer than forty saints. When her earthly remains were dug up to be placed in the chapel of the Carmelite monastery, those standing near her grave immediately smelled the aroma of roses! And her popularity spread so quickly that contributions from around the world helped fund the construction of the Basilica of Saint Thérèse, located in Lisieux, France.

Jesus said to his apostles: "Let the little ones come unto me." Saint Thérèse accepted this invitation by doing the "little things" that would eventually result in her assumption to the glory of God.

The Perfect "10"

Let me guess. You are not going to be a religious. You are not interested in becoming a martyr. And you are sure your resumé will not list miraculous encounters with heavenly agents. You could be right. However, the call to perfection must begin with a commitment that you will do your best to honor Jesus' call. "A new commandment I give to you, that you love one another; even as I have loved you, so you also love one another. By this all men will know that you are my disciples, if you have love for one another" (Jn 13:34–35).

To accomplish your mission, the following ten opportunities will get you where your soul wants to go.

1. Parents: Deliver the unexpected. Take out the trash before you are asked. Clean Dad's car. Do the dishes, though it is not your "responsibility". Be obedient even if their No seems unfair. Remember they love you. Clean your room without being asked. Inquire as to how you might make their day a little better. Love them. Forgive them. Pray for them.

2. Teachers: Give them a break. It is not easy to motivate a class of teenagers, many of whom are not interested. Offer to help after class. Never try to show them up. They are only human, just like you. Be professional when stating your position, avoiding unnecessary and unproductive confrontation. Love them. Forgive them. Pray for them.

3. Brothers/Sisters: "Blood is thicker than water." Do not take it lightly. Today's stupid brother is tomorrow's best friend. Today's selfish sister is tomorrow's confidant. Share with them. Listen to them. Reach out to them. Encourage them. Surprise them with your kindness. Love them. Forgive them. Pray for them.

4. Coaches: Sometimes they are not fair. Sometimes life is not fair. And sometimes you are not fair. Whether athletic, debate, theater, or academic coaches, they have a job to do. So do you. Work hard. Give your best. Help your teammates. Cheer the ones who put you on the bench. Go the extra mile after the race is over. Love them. Forgive them. Pray for them.

5. Friends: Some will last forever; others will come and go. What you do in these relationships may well

determine what they do with their lives. Never under-estimate the power of memories, good or bad. Some friends will break your heart, use you, betray you, confuse you. Love them. Forgive them. Pray for them.

6. Relatives: There will always be the "strange" one in the extended family. And sooner or later, grand-mother's or grandfather's mind will slip. Remember how they used to play with you, bring you gifts, and take you places? Now all they are asking is that you do not forget them. They did not forget you. Their time may be short. Do not add to their loneliness, it will only expedite their death. Some day you will be in their shoes. Love them. Forgive them. Pray for them.

7. Strangers: It is not easy. Some are odd. Some do not fit. Do not rush to judgment as David did in the Annunciation chapter. To this day, he wishes he had that moment back. You never know who the stranger might be who is asking for help. Love them. Forgive them. Pray for them.

8. Religious: There will always be "boring" priests, un-sophisticated nuns, and other representatives of the Church whose views do not match yours. But before you judge their behavior, take inventory of yours. Maybe you are the one who is boring. Perhaps your idea of "religion" is skewing your perception of what is really important. Give them a chance. Jesus did as much with twelve very "poor" students. Love them. Forgive them. Pray for them.

9. Neighbors: They may not share your interest. They may be different. But so are you. Respect them. Go the extra mile to let them know that young people can

be terrific citizens. Surprise them with your initiative. Smile. Stop by and say hello. Wish them a nice day. Offer to help if you notice they could use some. Love them. Forgive them. Pray for them.

10. Employers: All they want is a fair day's work for a fair day's pay. There will be times when you get the "dirty" work, the Friday night hours, the worst person to work with. Set an example. Do your best. Avoid complaining. Give the boss a chance; he gave you one. Show them what work ethic is all about. Love them. Forgive them. Pray for them.

Love, forgiveness, and prayer are the first three steps in your heavenly assumption. But remember, the journey to God begins with the little things. Take care of these, and God will take care of you.

The Little Mother

The author of the "Little Way" had a very special admirer whom she would never meet. Her name was Agnes Gonxha Bojaxhiu, better known as Mother Teresa. Born August 26, 1910, in Macedonia, she was one of three children. When she was twelve, she felt a calling to serve God by becoming a religious. When she was eighteen, she fulfilled that dream by joining the Sisters of Our Lady of

Loreto. She chose her name after the famous saint of Lisieux.

In December 1928, she began her journey to India to continue her religious training. Arriving in Calcutta on January 6, 1929, she was assigned to teach at a local Catholic girls high school. But her real calling was about to begin, as she could not turn her attention away from the sick and dying on Calcutta's streets. She would roam the streets, seeing where poor little children lived and what they ate. She soon became known as "Ma" by the local families.

On September 10, 1946, a date later referred to as Inspiration Day, she had a "life-changing" event. Mother Teresa was on a train en route to a retreat when God touched her heart. She had to leave the convent to help the poorest of the poor and live among them. She would recall how this seemed to pierce her soul. Following that spiritual experience, Mother Teresa asked permission to leave the Loreto congregation and establish a new order of sisters, the Missionaries of Charity. In 1952, Mother Teresa and a small handful of sisters began caring for India's "untouchables".

Over the years, this remarkable little sister shocked the world with her unconditional love, her firm stance in support of the poor and the unborn, and her profound humility. On September 5, 1997, Mother Teresa left this world. One can only imagine her meeting with her old friend and mentor, Sister Thérèse of Lisieux. But before she left, the little four-foot, eleven-inch sister from Albania had accomplished what few in the history of the world have done.

In just over fifty years of service she and her sisters

cared for more than forty thousand citizens from the streets of Calcutta, half of whom died in an atmosphere of kindness and love. One of her first "customers" was a woman half eaten by rats and ants. Mother Teresa carried her to a hospital where at first she was denied care. But after the sister refused to leave until the dying woman got medical attention, the hospital staff reluctantly took the woman in and cared for her. Because of her persistence, the local authorities gave her a shelter, which eventually became known as the "Home for the Dying Destitutes".

Another home was started for those children who had no parents to care for them. Some of the children came from the streets, others from hospitals where parents abandoned them. Many were sick or handicapped. Today there are over forty such houses just in India.

A third population Mother Teresa cared for was comprised of lepers. This group of poor souls lived like "dogs" in a culture where to be a leper was to be feared and shunned. Though she met with great resistance, Mother Teresa was able to convince the populace that many of the lepers could be healed and lead productive lives. One survivor is now a doctor who works in the streets of Calcutta.

But of all her contributions, perhaps the greatest was her defense of the unborn. Her philosophy can be easily summed up in one short statement. "The life of a child that still has to be born or the life of the poor whom we meet in the streets of Calcutta, Rome or anywhere else in the world, the life of children or adults is the same life. It is our life, it is a gift of God." She goes on to say: "Countries that allow abortion are poor, because they do not have the courage to accept one more life."

Mother Teresa's works have spread all over the world with her sisters serving alcoholics, drug addicts, the homeless, those with AIDS, orphans, prisoners, the poor, the dying, and the destitute. Even Pope John Paul II asked for her help, requesting that she establish homes for mothers with unwanted pregnancies.

Mother Teresa received numerous awards, including the Pope John XXIII Peace Prize; the Angel of Charity designation from the president of India; the Albert Schweitzer International award; the Nobel Peace Prize; and the Honorary Citizen of America award—she is one of only four people to receive this award.

Anyone who knew Mother Teresa, however, knew that honors, praise, and other worldly celebrations were unimportant to this woman, who was even called a "living saint". What was important was what she did for the children of God, especially those who were forgotten. She once said, "It is fashionable to talk about the poor. Unfortunately it is not fashionable to talk with them." She went on to say: "The poor are Christ Himself, and when we touch the sick and needy, we touch the suffering body of Christ."

Saint Thérèse of Lisieux, like her "protégé" Mother Teresa, did little things. But these little things became big things. Is that not what the assumption calls for?

THE CORONATION

"She who crushes the serpent"

IN the sixteenth century, Aztec Indians were involved in human sacrifice to the "feathered serpent god", Quetzalcoatl (pronounced ket-sal-ko-attle). It was a dark time in their history. Every year as many as fifty thousand men, women, and children were sacrificed to this pagan god. But after the Spanish explorer Cortez conquered Mexico, Christianity began to spread slowly.

One of the baptized Indians was Juan Diego. On December 9, 1531, this convert experienced a profound encounter with heaven. While on his way to Mass, he was passing Tepayac hill when all of a sudden he saw a brilliant light on the summit and heard music and then a woman's voice inviting him to approach. When he reached the top of the hill he was startled to see the Blessed Virgin Mary. As he fell on his knees the holy lady requested that he go to the bishop and ask that a temple be built where she could offer her love and protection.

Juan hurried down the hill to meet the bishop. But he was met with extreme skepticism. Dejected, Juan returned to the holy lady, begging her to select someone who could convince the bishop that the Mother of God had indeed visited the people of Mexico. Gently, Mary responded, "No. You will please go tomorrow and ask again." The next day Juan pleaded with the priest to come and see for himself. This time the bishop asked for proof that the Blessed Mother was appearing to a humble peasant. Returning to the top of the hill, Juan fell on his knees before the beautiful lady and told her of the bishop's request. "Very well", she said. "Come tomorrow, and I will give you all the proof the bishop needs."

But the following day Juan chose to stay with his uncle, who was very ill. The next day, December 12, Juan ran toward the town to get a priest who would give the last rites to his dying uncle. As he was racing past Tepayac Hill, the Virgin again appeared to him and said: "Do not worry about your uncle. He is already cured. Go to the mountain, take the flowers you find there, and bring them to me." Juan did what he was told and gathered some of the most beautiful roses he had ever seen. When he brought the flowers to the lady, she rearranged them in his tilma, allowing Juan to carry them to town. Returning to the bishop, Juan opened his tilma. But when the flowers fell to the floor the real miracle occurred. Inside Juan Diego's tilma was a beautiful image of the Blessed Mother. Both Juan and the bishop would later learn that the Mother of

God had appeared to Juan's uncle, curing him and asking that the image be given the title "Santa Maria de Guadalupe". The name means "She who crushes the serpent".

Juan Diego's famous tilma has been on display for almost five hundred years in Tepayac, near Mexico City. Millions of pilgrims have come to visit the Basilica to see the mystical portrait of our Lady. Many pagans soon converted, and this miraculous image is seen as a powerful testimonial for the entire world.

The image of the Blessed Mother is not the only miracle. Though the tilma is made of cactus, with a life expectancy of thirty years, the cloth has lasted fifteen times longer with no apparent wear or tear, even though it was totally unprotected from candle smoke, incense, and human touch for 117 years. Scientific tests have proven that the image does not have a single brush stroke, confirming that the image was not painted. Chemical analysis has determined that the color is not from animal, mineral, or vegetable origin. How the image was created remains a mystery. The roses depicted on the tilma are Castilian roses, grown only in Spain. There are forty-six stars on the gown, making up fourteen distinct constellations, all of which are in the precise positions that occurred on December 12, 1531. But the most startling discovery occurred during the magnification of our Lady's eyes, where one can clearly see the face of a man and his shoulders. The man seems to be Juan Diego, as he appears from an original painting of the Aztec Indian.

Science aside, there are signs that only the Aztec culture would understand. Our Lady is surrounded by the sun's rays, yet her image is hiding the sun. This told the superstitious Aztecs that she was more powerful than their sun god. Our Lady is standing on a burned-out crescent, a symbol of defeat for the dreaded serpent god of human sacrifice. Our Lady is dressed in a blue and green robe, symbolic of royalty. The stars on her robe communicated to the Indians that this woman was more powerful than any of the stars they worshipped. The black cross she is wearing resembles the same cross the Indians saw on the sails of Cortez, suggesting that the heavenly visitor is representing Christianity. The lady has her hands folded and head bowed in reverence to one far more important than she.

The power of Our Lady of Guadalupe's intercession can be measured by the sheer number of conversions that took place after the apparitions. In fifteen years more than nine million Indians were baptized. Today she is recognized as the Patroness of the Americas. And as a reminder to all who would sacrifice their children, our Lady is "Patroness of the Unborn". As further testimony to God's plan of redemption, one need only read Revelation 12:1. "A great portent appeared in heaven, a woman clothed with the sun, with the moon under her feet, and on her head a crown of twelve stars." Though it was written almost two thousand years ago, the fulfillment of the prophecy has escalated with every Marian apparition. There are those who have seen and shared their encounter with the Mother of God; and there are those who have not seen but have chosen to believe in her message. Both groups can be assured that "a woman clothed with the sun" will be present at their coronation.

"Quo Vadis?"

The Latin phrase means, "Where are you going?" Bernadette was on her way to pick up firewood when our Lady intervened. Francis of Assisi wanted to be a soldier but ended up in the Army of God. Joan of Arc was a peasant girl who led an army of soldiers. Aloysius was a young man who traded his right to the king's court for the court of heaven. Saints Agnes and Maria Goretti chose good over evil, and through their sacrifice many souls have been saved. Kateri and Germaine, once marked with physical imperfections, are now perfect in the eyes of God. Father John Vianney, the priest originally forbidden to hear confessions, has become the Patron Saint for Confessors worldwide. The Apostles John and Peter were nothing more than fishermen who would eventually become "fishers of men".

Saint Joseph was a poor carpenter whose foundation of faith helped raise the Son of God. John of the Cross wrote the *Dark Night of the Soul*, which was once condemned. The poem is now one of the most popular mystical writings ever published. Maximilian Kolbe wanted to serve God by loving his neighbor. He was canonized a saint because he gave his life for that neighbor. Edith Stein was a Jewish intellectual who used her intellect to follow the Way of the Cross. She died in Auschwitz. Isaac Jogues, John Gabriel Perboyre, and Charles Lwanga sacrificed their lives so that those who killed them might one day gain eternal life. Sister Faustina asked for mercy and was rewarded by the King of Mercy! Michael the Archangel protected heaven. He now protects its future residents. The "Little Flower" had such a simple way of doing things that she is now one of the most celebrated saints in the Church.

"But they are saints of God", you say. Remember the story of David and his encounter with the angel? His life changed because he knew it had to. What about John, the salesman who needed a sign? He got it! Now he carries a big sign for God. Paul Rundi continues to journey toward his final "epiphany". Kaye O'Bara remains faithful to her eternal promise. Danny is "living" the fruits of his discernment. Gianna, Rebecca, Brenda, Carol, and Sarah are soldiers in the battle to defend the "sanctity of life". Padre Pio bore the wounds of Christ so that others might join Him in heaven. Monsignor Hugh O'Flaherty, like fellow priest Gereon Goldmann, stood his ground in the face of evil. More than half a century later, their courage has been celebrated in book, video, and film. Karol Wojtyla once said, "It is too early for a Polish Pope." Two days later the world was introduced to Pope John Paul II. Larry Vuillemin, the man who was angry at God, found that God had forgiven him for his misguided anger. Coach Gerry Faust discovered that his real calling was not winning games, but winning souls. Father Joseph became the priest whom many priests said he would never be. Father John Corapi gave up the material riches of this world for eternal riches in the next. And Mother Teresa, winner of the Nobel Peace Prize, has won an even greater prize.

Where are you going? Are you willing to show the Mother of God that you want to do the will of her Son? If you do, you are ready for your annunciation. Will you be charitable toward your neighbor? If so, prepare for your visitation. Are you ready for your "awakening"? Your epiphany is not far behind. Are you willing to give all you have to Him who gives you all you need? When you do your consecration will begin. Do you admit to knowing the difference between right and wrong, good and evil? And will you act accordingly? The gift of discernment demands as much. Our Lady is waiting for your PROMISE.

Where are you going? Are you sorry for your sins? Come to Gethsemane. Will you stand up for what is right? Public scourging is imminent. Do you have courage? The crown of ridicule awaits you. Can you persevere? Many are waiting to see if you will help them carry their cross. Will your moral fortitude strengthen your convictions? Prepare for the crucifixion of truth. Fear not, our Lady will be with you in your time of PASSION.

Where are you going? Do you believe in Jesus, the Son of God? Your resurrection is approaching. Are you ready for a higher calling? The hour of your ascension is near. Will you invite the Holy Spirit into your life? Your Pentecost has arrived. Will you "live" the rosary? Your assumption toward His Mother will guarantee your assumption toward her Son. Both are waiting for your coronation. And when that day comes, our Lady will be there to celebrate your PURIFICATION.

Quo Vadis? The choice is yours.

"Do Not Be Afraid, Mary, for You Have Found Favor with God"

The passage is from Luke 1:30. Mary was a young teenager when she heard these words from the Angel Gabriel. If that was not enough, she soon learned that she was chosen to be the Mother of the Son of God! Her response changed eternity. "Behold, I am the handmaid of the Lord. May it be done to me according to your word." From that moment on, the Blessed Virgin Mary had joined her Son in His quest to save the world from sin.

Over the centuries Mary has appeared to many people. All were invited to accept God's invitation. Mary would do exactly what the Angel Gabriel did. She would first comfort the startled "visionary" and then announce that he had been chosen for a very special assignment.

You will recall the story of Bernadette Soubirous, the teenager who saw our Lady in a grotto near the town's city dump. The location was not exactly where one would expect the Queen of Heaven to visit. But then again, Mary was the Queen who gave birth to a King in a stable, where the only signs of royalty were in the hearts of the poor shepherds. Juan Diego's status was not much different when he encountered Our Lady of Guadalupe. In both cases, Mary appeared to simple souls whose faith led to the conversions of tens of thousands.

There have been others who "found favor with God".

On May 13, 1917, at the height of World War I, three children from Fatima, Portugal—Lucia, Francisco, and Jacinta, ages ten, nine, and seven, respectively—were busy tending sheep. Suddenly, a bright ball of light came to rest atop a small tree. Out of the ball appeared a beautiful lady. She was the Blessed Mother, who had come to ask the children if they would be willing to visit with her on the same day for six consecutive months. Before her first visit ended, our Lady had one request: "Pray the rosary every day to obtain peace for the world and the end of the war." Shortly thereafter, the children were ridiculed by family and friends and threatened by the authorities for spreading lies about a heavenly visitor. The children remained faithful, returning to the same spot where the Lady had first appeared. With each successive apparition, more and more people began to accompany the three seers. And though only the children could see and hear the Lady, the crowd began to sense that God had chosen Fatima for some very special purpose. They were right.

During our Lady's second visit, she said to the children: "Jesus wishes to establish devotion to my Immaculate Heart." At the third apparition, she again asked the children to pray for the end of the war. It was also during this visit that she showed the children a glimpse of hell. Lucia would state in later years that were it not for the Blessed Mother's promise to take them to heaven, all three of them would have died of fright.

There was another prophecy shared that day. Our Lady told the children that all should pray for the consecration of Russia to her Immaculate Heart. At the time this request was made, the home of communism was spreading the errors of its ways throughout the world. The warning was clear. If the request was not honored, many nations would suffer under communist rule. Eventually, our Lady promised, Russia would be converted.

During the fourth apparition, our Lady asked the people of Fatima to build a chapel at the site of the visitations. Though the chapel was built, enemies of the Church destroyed the structure some two years later. Today, the Basilica of Fatima is visited by hundreds of thousands of pilgrims from all over the world who come to pray at the magnificent shrine.

At the fifth apparition, our Lady continued to ask the people to pray the rosary. In attendance were more than twenty thousand faithful. And then the Mother of God made another promise. "In October, I will perform a miracle for all to believe." That miracle occurred on October 13, 1917, in front of seventy thousand people. It became known as "the miracle of the sun". After it had rained all day, the sun suddenly appeared and began to spin, spewing forth vibrant colors. All the people were able to stare at the dancing sun without hurting their eyes. After about ten minutes, the sun appeared to return to its original place. Much to the people's shock, their clothes, soaked from the pouring rain, were dry!

Fatima, Lourdes, and Guadalupe are some of the most popular shrines in the world, yet there are others. In Paris, France, on July 18, 1830, twenty-four-year-old Sister Catherine Labouré was startled in the middle of her sleep to see a young child standing next to her bed. The little boy said, "Sister Catherine, the Blessed Virgin awaits you." When the boy led the young nun to the chapel, Sister Catherine found the entire room aglow. There the Holy Mother prepared this future saint for a special assignment. There would be several appearances over the coming months. Then on November 27, the first Sunday of Advent, Sister Catherine received a visualization of a medal. On one side were the words, "O Mary, conceived without sin, pray for us who have recourse to thee." The words surrounded an image of the Blessed Virgin Mary. On the reverse side was a large "M" with a bar and cross on top. Below the symbol were the hearts of Jesus and Mary, one crowned with thorns, the other pierced by the sword. The Blessed Mother then said: "Have a medal struck according to this model. Those who wear it after being blessed shall receive great graces, especially if they wear it around their neck. Graces will be abundant for those who have confidence." Within five years more than two million medals had been distributed throughout Paris. Though it is officially called the Medal of the Immaculate Conception, so many spiritual conversions and bodily cures have occurred that the medal has become known as the Miraculous Medal.

Other alleged apparitions have occurred around the world. Some of the more well known are La Salette, France; Knock, Ireland; Beauraing, Belgium; Akita, Japan; Garabandal, Spain; Kibeho, Africa; Betania, Venezuela; and Medjugorje, Bosnia. Throughout the world, devotion to the Mother of God is commonplace. Africa, Asia, the Holy Land, Europe, and the Americas all have shrines or basilicas named in honor of the Blessed Virgin Mary. Regardless of continent, culture, approved apparition site, or shrine, the single most common request associated with the Blessed Mother is for all God's children to return to Him through faith, prayer, conversion, fasting, penance, and reconciliation. Follow her petition, and you too will find favor with God.

Saints Bernadette, Joan of Arc, Maria Goretti, and countless others answered her call a long time ago. In more recent times, Mother Teresa, Padre Pio, Saint Maximilian Kolbe, and Pope John Paul II have all demonstrated their love for God. Today, our Lady's army includes the single mother who continues to care for her comatose daughter; the retired football coach who will never retire from the love of God; the young attorney whose mother chose not to abort her daughter; the angry priest who needed the warmth of the Blessed Mother; the teacher who was taught to serve God through love of family and students; the father of ten adopted children whose gift in life is to share his faith with other parents. Also included are the salesman who now gives away his love for Christ; the lawyer whose anger at God has since been refocused on the Immaculate Heart of Mary and the Sacred Heart of Jesus; the priest who traded his worldly sins for heavenly mercy—and the author of this book, whose encounter in a chapel led to a greater commitment to Jesus and His Blessed Mother.

Mary has another invitation: She is reaching out to her children throughout the world. She asks that you join her in preparation for the second coming of her Son. She asks that you say prayers that invite the Holy Spirit into your life. She requests that you receive the sacraments, attend Mass, obey the commandments, and pray the rosary. She is pleading that you will make this promise to her and her Son. And she promises that if you do, paradise will be yours.

Why would this sinless Virgin play such an important role in your salvation? The answer lies in Holy Scripture. In Genesis 3:15, God warns Satan, "I will put enmity between you and the woman, and between your seed and her seed." Adam and Eve were deceived by the devil, resulting in the stain of original sin. The new Eve is Mary, the Immaculate Conception, whose "offspring" is Jesus, the Son of God. Together they will crush the head of the serpent. In Revelation 12:17, there is further testimony to good versus evil. "Then the dragon [serpent] was angry with the woman, and went off to make war on the rest of her offspring, on those who keep the commandments of God and bear testimony to Jesus."

In Search of Mary

To know Mary is to know the virtues identified with the Mother of Jesus. Humility, love for God, love for her neighbor, faith, hope, chastity, poverty, obedience, patience, and prayer represent a highly desirable road for you to follow.

To know Mary is to recognize the sorrows she experienced. Simeon the prophet told the Holy Mother that one day her Son's Passion and death would pierce her heart. She had to flee to Egypt to prevent her child from being killed. She lost her twelve-year-old Son for three days during the busiest festival of the year. She had to say goodbye to Jesus, knowing He was going to His execution. She would then witness His death. She saw a soldier drive a lance into her Son's side to ensure that He was dead. And, finally, this tender Mother would bury her Son. To understand these sorrows is to accept how much the Savior's Mother loves her children.

To know Mary is to study why the saints honored her;

why so many books have been written about her; why hundreds of thousands of people recite her rosary daily; why theologians continue to study her life; why so many children have reported seeing her; why shrines all over the world have been built in her honor; and why the Catholic Church celebrates her life no fewer than fifteen times each calendar year.

To know Mary is to know the Litany of Loreto, with its titles and invocations. Learn why we ask: Mother of God, Virgin of virgins, Mother of Christ, Mother of divine grace, Mother most pure, Mother most chaste, Mother inviolate, Mother undefiled, Mother most amiable, Mother most admirable, Mother of good counsel, Mother of our Creator, and Mother of our Savior, pray for us. Learn why this Virgin is referred to as most prudent, venerable, renowned, powerful, merciful, and faithful. Discover the meaning behind her titles: Mirror of Justice, Seat of Wisdom, Cause of Our Joy, Spiritual Vessel, Vessel of Honor, Singular Vessel of Devotion, Mystical Rose, Tower of David, Tower of Ivory, House of Gold, Ark of the Covenant, Gate of Heaven, Morning Star, Health of the Sick, Refuge of Sinners, Comforter of the Afflicted, and Help of Christians. Uncover the reasons why Mary is known as Queen of angels, patriarchs, prophets, apostles, martyrs, confessors, virgins, and saints. Learn the meaning behind the Litany of Loreto and you will come to understand the meaning behind the phrases "Queen conceived without original sin", "Queen assumed into heaven", "Queen of the most holy rosary", and "Queen of peace".

Finally, to know Mary is to believe in the fifteen promises to those who recite the rosary. These promises, as reported by Saint Dominic and Blessed Alan de la Roche, are as follows:

1. Whoever recites the rosary shall receive singular graces.
2. I promise special protection and graces to those who recite the rosary.
3. The rosary will destroy vice, decrease sin, and defeat heresies.
4. The rosary will cause virtue and good works to flourish; it will obtain for souls the abundant mercy of God; it will withdraw the hearts of people from the love of the world and its vanities and will lift them to the desire of eternal things.
5. The souls of those who recite the rosary shall not perish.
6. Those who recite the rosary devoutly shall never be conquered by misfortune; God will not chastise them in His justices; they shall not perish by an unprovided death; if they be just, they shall remain in the grace of God and become worthy of eternal life.
7. Those who have a true devotion to the rosary shall not die without the sacraments of the Church.
8. Those who are faithful in the recitation of the rosary shall have, during their life and at their death, the light of God and the plenitude of His graces; at the moment of death they shall participate in the merits of the saints in paradise.
9. I shall deliver from Purgatory those who have been devoted to the rosary.
10. The faithful children of the rosary shall merit a high degree of glory in heaven.

11. You shall obtain all that you ask of me by the recitation of the rosary.

12. All those who propagate the holy rosary shall be aided by me in their necessities.

13. I have obtained from my divine Son that all the advocates of the rosary shall have for intercessors the entire celestial court during their life and at the hour of their death.

14. All who recite the rosary are my children, and brothers and sisters of my only Son, Jesus Christ.

15. Devotion of my rosary is a sign of predestination.

The choice to give Mary your heart is yours. If you do so choose, the words *Salve, Regina* will mean everything to you. And to help you understand their meaning, the following prayer is left for you to ponder. It is the time of your Desiderata.

Hail, holy Queen, Mother of Mercy: hail, our life, our sweetness and our hope. To you do we cry, poor banished children of Eve. To you do we send up our sighs, mourning and weeping in this valley of tears. Turn, then, most gracious advocate, your eyes of mercy toward us. And after this, our exile, show unto us the blessed fruit of your womb, Jesus. O clement, O loving, O sweet Virgin Mary.

Epilogue

DESIDERATA

As you continue your journey to God, remember what peace there is in prayer. Through your personal conversations, whether in laughter, tears, or silence, never forget that your Creator is listening. Do what you must to warrant the respect and love of others, both friend and foe. God has given you the title "Christian". Make sure you earn it. When you do not have time to give to those who fail to meet *your* standards, these will be the times when you fail to meet God's! Listen to your conscience, the tapestry of your guardian angel. God sent you this spiritual being for a reason. Satan sends his minions for other reasons. Be sure you discern the difference. Enjoy your achievements, as well as your dreams. But keep in touch with the Holy Spirit. He may have other plans for you. For what He will bring to the table will satisfy your eternal hunger. Rest assured, there will be times of difficulty or sudden misfortune. Do not wait till then to talk with God. Remember the saints. Trust in Him whom they trusted. They faced trials. You will too. And though the world is full of trickery, be not blind to what is good in life. Strive for high ideals. Raise the bar. Sooner or later God will ask you to lead a new crusade. Have courage. Have conviction. Have faith. Never forget those who love you. Forgive those who have forgotten you. Reach out to the same hands that held your hand when you were first learning to walk. You once needed them. They need you now. Remember, God loves you. He always did. He always will.

That is why He sent His Son. That is why Jesus sends His Mother. And that is why she is asking you to prepare for the Holy Spirit. For whether you know it or not, there are big plans for you. All you need do is promise that, first, you "will seek the kingdom of heaven". All you need is passion. The kind of passion that will help you deliver the promise you made to God. All you need is purification. With a clean heart, mind, and soul, your coronation is in sight. And when that hour arrives, you will most certainly hear these words: "Well done, good and faithful servant. For you multiplied in the lives of others those talents I gave you. And as you loved My Son, His Blessed Mother, and My Holy Spirit, so too do I love you. Welcome home!"

AUTHOR'S RECOMMENDATIONS

Books, Videos, and Tapes

There are many fine Catholic publishers who offer a variety of materials that teens and their parents will find of interest. Ignatius Press offers Catholic books, videos, cassettes, and CD-ROMs. These include books on saints, Father John Corapi tapes, and inspirational videos. Some books I highly recommend include *The Shadow of His Wings*, by Fr. Gereon Goldmann; *Saints for Now*, by Clare Boothe Luce; and Mark Twain's *Joan of Arc*. Other Ignatius Press books that may be of interest are *Life Work*, by Rick Sarkesian (also on video); *Real Love* and *We're on a Mission from God*, both by Mary Beth Bonacci; and *Saints for Today*, by Ivan Innerst. (For a copy of their free catalog, call 1-800-651-1531 or visit www.Ignatius.com.)

Another organization worth knowing is Our Sunday Visitor. *Ordinary Suffering of Extraordinary Saints* is a terrific book highlighting men and women who faced multiple trials on their way to sainthood. (To get a complete listing of all their books, call 1–800–348–2440. You can also pick up their weekly newspaper in many Catholic church vestibules.)

Tan Books and Publishers, Rockford, Illinois, is known for some outstanding books on the saints. A few examples are *Secular Saints*, by Joan Carroll Cruz, and *A Year with the Saints*, by the Sisters of Mercy, Hartford, Connecticut. These books will add to your understanding of, and appreciation for, these heroes of the Church. (For a listing of all their publications, call 1–800–437–5876.)

Another book I highly recommend is *Fifty-Seven Saints*, by Eileen Heffernan, Pauline Books and Media, Boston, Massachusetts. The author has selected a number of saints whose stories are both entertaining and inspirational.

In the book entitled *The Saints, Humanly Speaking* (Servant Publications, 2000), Felicitas Corrigan has compiled 114 letters personally written by saints. To quote the author, "In the letters of the saints, our heroic brothers and sisters in Christ, we find wit, wisdom, pain, fear, joy . . . all the emotions of our common humanity." (Again, you can order the book on-line or through your bookstore.)

If the story of Kaye O'Bara and her daughter, Edwarda, touched your heart, you may want to order *A Promise Is a Promise*, by the noted author and public speaker Dr. Wayne W. Dyer. The title of his book says it all. (To order, call Hay House, Inc. at 1–800–654–5126.) Another book that treats one of the examples in this present work in greater depth is *The Golden Dream*, by Coach Gerry Faust and Steve Love. The true story of the ex-Notre Dame coach will put in perspective what is really important in life. (The publisher is Sports Publishing, Champaign, Illinois.)

Locate the Catholic bookstore nearest to you, and you will find numerous books, videos, tapes, and a variety of religious articles. Books such as Kevin Orlin Johnson's *Rosary, Mysteries, Meditations, and the Telling of the Beads* will provide you with both the history and the purpose of the rosary. Sister Faustina's *Divine Mercy Diary* and other books on the Blessed Mother are available for those who want to get to know the Mother of God, her Son, Jesus, and the saints who love them both. If you want to read about the Holy Father, there is no greater source than George Weigel's book *Witness to Hope: The Biography of Pope John Paul II*, published by Cliff Street Books.

Two other books on Mary are worth noting. *The Essential Mary Handbook* and *The Glories of Mary* are excellent resources for a better understanding of the vital role of the Blessed Virgin Mother. Both books are published by Liguori Publications. An important and informative book is the *Catechism of the Catholic Church*. Every Catholic home should have a copy available.

In this world of internet travel, you are limited only by time, desire, and imagination. To that end, I challenge you to start searching for those organizations and materials that will provide the resources necessary to strengthen your faith.

Finally, if the readers of this book would like to experience the *Desiderata Workshop Series*, they may send an e-mail to me at DPE22@aol.com, and I will mail out a program brochure listing presentations and workshops for teens and adults.

Jesus said: "Seek and you shall find. Knock and it will be opened to you." Enjoy your *Desiderata*.